Andrew Carnegie

ANDREW CARNEGIE'S PEACE ENDOWMENT

ENDOWMENT

The Tycoon, The President, and Their Bargain of 1910

by

Larry L. Fabian

Œ

Carnegie Endowment for International Peace
Washington, D.C.
1985

ISBN 0-87003-040-X
Library of Congress Catalog Card Number: 85-71392
Printed in the United States of America

*F*oreword

On anniversaries thoughts turn easily to history, and as the Carnegie Endowment approached its seventy-fifth, we felt that our friends and former associates might enjoy a glimpse into how it all began. Andrew Carnegie gave $10 million in 1910 to set up the Endowment. Retelling the story of why he did it would be, we assumed, a relatively straightforward job. Over many years assorted historians have written about the Endowment's origins. Several decades ago an internal history was compiled in two fact-packed volumes. The archives of the Endowment's early years have long been available to scholars at the library of Columbia University.

But for reasons none of us initially suspected—least of all Endowment Secretary Larry Fabian, who had agreed to pull a little information together for the occasion—the glimpse we had intended to provide has turned into an original and serious piece of history. For the story was not straightforward at all. It appeared, in fact, to be something of a puzzle, and the more we looked into it, the more ill-fitting the pieces seemed. Three conspicuously unanswered questions were not addressed satisfactorily in the available accounts of the Endowment's beginnings.

The first was why Carnegie waited until almost the end of his philanthropic years before endowing an organization to promote international peace. One would have expected that a man so strongly committed to peace would have placed the creation of an organization like the Carnegie Endowment at or near the top of his money-giving agenda. But he took the step only after all of his other large single-purpose benefactions had already been established during the first decade of this century.

The second question was why Carnegie seemed so aloof from the Endowment. In all of his major trusts, he left wide and proper discretion to his trustees. But he characteristically involved himself actively in the formative periods of overall policy setting for his new benefactions. Not so, however, with the Carnegie Endowment, according to the picture provided by the conventional historical accounts.

The third question was the most puzzling. Why did so pragmatic a man, a man whose astonishing successes in business rested on attention to detail and insistence on practical results, why did this man create an organization with so abstract and quixotic a mission as to rid the world of war?

These three questions yielded answers only after we realized that the story could not merely be retold. It had to be redis-covered, unearthed by a fresh look into the private papers of the principals, the history of their times, and the archives of the Endowment.

Carnegie's sense of his own destiny was more than ample. Lover of Shakespeare that he was, he probably would have seen himself in these lines from *Henry IV:*

> There is a history in all men's lives,
> Figuring the nature of the times
>   deceas'd,
> The which observ'd, a man may
>   prophesy,
> With a near aim, of the main
>   chance of things
> As yet not come to life, which in
>   their seeds
> And weak beginnings lie
>   intreasured.

Seventy-five years ago the "seeds" and "weak beginnings" of American internationalism were very much in evidence. Carnegie's decision to create the Endowment was intensely personal and calculated. It revealed much about those "times deceas'd" when the makers of American foreign policy were first struggling to come to terms with their country's emergence as a world power. It was a struggle to determine whether peaceful diplomacy or reliance on military power would define the character of an American internationalism-in-the-making. It was a struggle that took concrete and specific shape in 1910 and 1911, and Carnegie wanted his new organization to affect the outcome.

With this appreciation of Carnegie's motives, the pieces to the puzzle fall into place. He waited until 1910 because only then did he see what he thought was a political opportunity to make a difference. He did not remain aloof once he made his decision; he immersed himself in minutiae. His private agenda was as practical as it was immediate, interesting not because it was visionary and melioristic, but precisely because it drew him and his organization into the center of a historic foreign-policy controversy.

Had the Tax Reform Act of 1969 existed in those days, with its restrictions against foundation lobbying and legislative advocacy, the story told in these pages would have deserved another, more sensational ending—indeed, a simpler ending, for it would have been a tale of simple illegality. What Carnegie did seventy-five years ago would not pass muster today if tested against the standards governing the political activities of private, tax-exempt foundations.

But then, those were simpler times.
Or were they?

Thomas L. Hughes, President
Carnegie Endowment for
International Peace

Andrew Carnegie's Political Bargain

Andrew Carnegie in 1913

November 4, 1910

Andrew Carnegie sends a handwritten note to his closest friend, the English Liberal John Morley: "Private. *I have a new idea, or rather I have decided once for all my course . . . upon a new idea— but will take some time before announced—President approves heartily so does Root.*"

Gone were the hesitations that had long prevented Carnegie from establishing an American organization dedicated to the promotion of peace. When urged to do so a decade earlier, he had rejected the advice unequivocally. "I do not see that it is wise to devote our efforts to creating another organization," he wrote then. "Of course I may be wrong in believing that, but I am certainly not wrong in believing that if it were dependent on any millionaire's money it would begin as an object of pity and end as one of derision." He warmed to his subject with one of those aphorisms that have become part of Carnegie lore: "There is nothing that robs a righteous cause of its strength more than a millionaire's money. Its life is tainted thereby."

Now, however, he was convinced. The time seemed ripe because the politics had suddenly become right. After all, the president who approved so heartily of Carnegie's new idea was William Howard Taft, whose foreign-policy program in 1910 had spurred Carnegie into action. Carnegie wanted Taft's blessing not just for window dressing or for the good public relations that Carnegie certainly valued as a long-time Republican party loyalist. What Carnegie really wanted was a working political bargain with the president. Taft's part of the bargain would be to press forward with a peace policy that he had hinted at earlier in the year. Carnegie wanted to see that policy produce an American-led effort to fashion an unprecedented network of treaties for the peaceful settlement of disputes among nations. Having favored such treaties for many years, Carnegie, for his part of the bargain, would set up an influential private organization to support the president's policy.

In the weeks after confiding cryptically to Morley, Carnegie was in close touch with Taft and his secretary of state, Philander C. Knox, a fellow Pennsylvanian and one-time lawyer for the Carnegie Steel Company. Carnegie asked them both to approve the deed of trust he had personally written for the new organization. Not even Carnegie's newly selected trustees were yet privy to the contents of the docu-

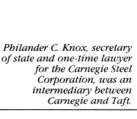

William Howard Taft and Elihu Root blessed Carnegie's new venture.

Philander C. Knox, secretary of state and one-time lawyer for the Carnegie Steel Corporation, was an intermediary between Carnegie and Taft.

ment. Carnegie also wanted the president to show early good faith on his part of the bargain by including in his next message to Congress language that would demonstrate presidential resolve to move definitively toward the preparation of treaties for negotiation. Taft finessed, telling Carnegie to talk the subject over with Knox, who would then prepare what he thought prudent for the message.

But the president was franker to a White House aide: "The trouble with old Carnegie is, he might secure what he wants in my message and then not give the money. I think I will go a little slow until old Andrew becomes more specific." Wary though he was, the president did nothing to discourage Carnegie, and readily accepted his invitation to become honorary president of the new organization.

Taft's name and official designation did not appear alongside those of other officers and trustees in the new organiza-

tion's first annual report in 1911. Anyone who might have noticed and who knew the unhappy fate of Carnegie's political bargain would have been neither surprised nor puzzled by the omission.

The other man who had given Carnegie an initial green light for his "new idea" was intimately involved in Carnegie's maneuvering with the president. That was Elihu Root, long-time arbiter of foreign-policy wisdom in Republican Washington. Root had entered government service as President William McKinley's secretary of war in 1899. After McKinley's assassination in 1901, he remained at the War Department in Theodore Roosevelt's cabinet and then became secretary of state during Roosevelt's second term. Admired at home and abroad as a statesman of extraordinary distinction, Root was entering the final years of his official career during the Taft administration of 1909-1913, having been chosen in 1909 to represent New

York State in the U.S. Senate. Root was then sixty-four. Although he had declined Taft's offer to stay on as secretary of state, he was considered one of the president's important early advisers on foreign policy. So high was Carnegie's regard for Root that the philanthropist attached one precondition to his plans for the new enterprise: Root must agree to lead it.

On December 14, 1910, a seventy-five-year-old Carnegie turned over to his assembled new trustees in Washington the sum of $10 million—in U.S. Steel bonds generating an annual income of $500,000. President of the Board Root and several trustees in the inner circle decided a few weeks later to name the benefaction the Carnegie Endowment for International Peace.

The story of the Carnegie Endowment's origins spans many years at the turn of this century. It involves a large cast of characters who presided over, argued about, and participated in America's passage from nineteenth-century insularity to twentieth-century globalism. To see the story whole requires empathy with men who in retrospect seem to us as innocent about the terrible phenomenon of modern war as they were about the elusive pathways to peace.

ANDREW CARNEGIE GIVES TEN MILLIONS TO PROMOTE PEACE THROUGHOUT WORLD

Makes Formal Transfer of Bonds to Trustees, Headed by Elihu Root.

The first entry in the Carnegie Endowment's cash journal: $10 million in U.S. Steel bonds

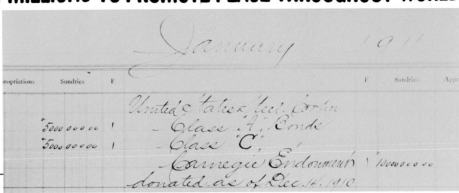

THE FOUNDER

Andrew Carnegie was a man whose contradictions were as vast as his wealth and were sometimes at war in his personality, his intellectual temperament, his scheme of social and moral values, and his politics. Charm, a gentle sense of humor, an honest humanity, an ingratiating impishness, and a kindliness of spirit, all of these he displayed in abundance. Yet he also possessed a boundless capacity for convincing himself that right was always on his side. Fortified by a herculean self-confidence and an outsized ego, he could be preachy and condescending. His spacious intellectual curiosity and the range of his reading and interests were truly impressive, a trait not uncommon among self-educated men. And he was vain enough to flaunt his distinctiveness among the normally less cerebral tycoons of his generation, once speculating that one of them would surely exchange millions for his knowledge of Shakespeare. Yet Carnegie's learning was broad rather than deep; impressionistic rather than rigorous. It tended to confirm his instincts and existing beliefs; to make him more certain rather than more skeptical.

His immense fortune was earned shrewdly and, when necessary, ruthlessly.

Yet his public persona and his lifestyle showed little of the mindless ostentation typical of other industrial captains from America's Gilded Age—as the era was christened by Mark Twain, one of Carnegie's most cherished personal friends. This Scottish immigrant of once-humble, even impoverished, circumstances devoted most of his life to making money, and when he sold his steel empire to J. P. Morgan in 1900, the imperious Wall Street entrepreneur journeyed up to Carnegie's East Ninety-first Street mansion and congratulated him on becoming the richest man in the world.

Carnegie, even by then, had become an item of authentic Americana for his promise to give away most of his fortune in his lifetime. And after 1900, he did. Philanthropy became his business and his topmost personal preoccupation. Faithful to his self-proclaimed "Gospel of Wealth," written in 1889, Carnegie acted out his conviction that the wealthy man who dies rich dies disgraced. Satirists found a tempting target. One published a "Constitution of Carnegia," a blueprint for a mythical utopia where rich, aging Carnegians furiously competed to dispense their fortunes for public good. Thus fulfilled, they could retire as "Honored Citizens," satisfied and secure in the knowledge that they

had earned their Carnegian constitutional right to be supported by the state for the rest of their lives "in extreme comfort."

Carnegie's world was a rarefied one of wealth, power, and privilege. His genuine sense of social justice, however, was advanced and sensitive, nourished since his youth by both personal experience and emotional commitment. His attachment to the radical politics of social reform in his native Scotland had roots deep in his family background.

His abhorrence of violence and hatred of war were passionate. He helped finance the anti-imperialist side in the rancorous domestic debate over American imperialism after the war with Spain in 1898. He opposed America's acquisition of the Philippines after Spain relinquished the territory, and he was appalled by his country's subsequent suppression of the Philippine independence movement. Yet he was able to justify war in practice. He never doubted that the Union cause in the American Civil War was justified in order to end slavery, and he even admitted that he saw some good come of the Spanish-American conflict inasmuch as it brought independence to Cuba. Throughout Carnegie's life, his pacifist sentiments were dominant, but an absolute pacifist he was not.

5

Carnegie's New York mansion, today the Cooper-Hewitt Museum

J. P. Morgan bought Carnegie's steel empire for $480 million.

His politically conservative, Republican credentials were almost never out of order. Even so, he identified himself with progressive causes during the Roosevelt years. He favored tighter regulation of banking and the railroads, as well as tougher measures to conserve natural resources. He urged tariff reform. And he lavishly praised Roosevelt's forward-looking leadership in promoting economic and social changes that most men of corporate wealth regarded as treacherous breaches of Republican faith.

Carnegie's beliefs were occasionally erratic, and they were never concealed. Unlike most magnates of the industrial age, he was a public man, reflective in temperament and driven by an urge to explain himself and his times to his contemporaries. It is impossible to imagine his being sympathetic to John D. Rockefeller's favored maxim, Silence is Golden. And never would Carnegie have answered the question "How do you feel this morning?" as the secretive king of Southern Pacific Railways, Leland Stanford, once did: "Wouldn't you like to know?"

A bulging legacy of books, articles, speeches, and letters provides an abundant but often fuzzy picture of Carnegie's thinking. His literary and rhetorical styles were frequently extravagant, idiosyncratic, and frustratingly elliptical. He was in many ways a simple man who deserved to be taken at face value, and in other ways a complicated figure acting out of some combination of impulse and bedrock conviction that not even his closest associates could discern clearly. Richard Watson Gilder, editor of the *Century Magazine* and Carnegie's greatly valued friend, once described him as "really a tremendous personality—dramatic, wilful, generous, whimsical, at times almost cruel in pressing his own conviction upon others, and then again tender, affectionate, emotional, always imaginative, unusual and wide-vi-

sioned in his views. He is well worth Boswellizing."

In all, Carnegie mirrored his age. A panoramic popular history of America during the first quarter of this century casts him as a virtual national symbol, a person who "in his ambition to be rich coupled with his impulse toward benevolence, his earnestness of reform, and his reverence toward education, was the average American of the time, apotheosized by success." He mirrored his age's serio-comic side, too, most notably, perhaps, in his quest for a simplified spelling system for the English language. The Carnegie treasure-house of curiosities included his financial backing of language-reform schemes, and he himself liked to write "hav" rather than "have," "tho" rather than "though," or "spelt" rather than "spelled." That just such reform, however, had been a passion of leading personalities of the day, and even of Roosevelt, who had tried once to impose a new spelling system on the U.S. government, is more often forgotten. For Twain, it was a perfect opportunity to needle his friend, and one can only guess at the prudish Carnegie's reaction to Twain's quip that simplified spelling was like chastity—a good thing as far as it goes, but capable of being carried too far.

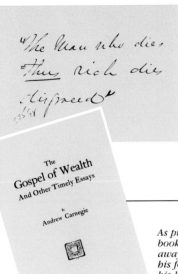

"The man who dies thus rich dies disgraced"

The
Gospel of Wealth
And Other Timely Essays

By
Andrew Carnegie

New York
The Century Co.
1901

As promised in this book, Carnegie gave away 90 per cent of his fortune during his lifetime.

Theodore Roosevelt, like Carnegie, supported "the simplified spelling movement." In the cartoon on the left, TR takes a few shots at the dictionary. The box is marked "amunishon from A. Carnegie." In the cartoon on the right, the King's English is unwelcome in Roosevelt's White House.

THE FOUNDER'S WISE MAN

Carnegie met with his new trustees for an hour and a half that December morning in 1910 and treated them to a vintage Carnegie performance. After reading his deed of trust, he told stories. Their point was simple: to underscore his supreme confidence in Root. Carnegie recounted two visits with Roosevelt at the White House, both with Root present. The first was a lunch at which Carnegie watched in admiration as Root deftly maneuvered Roosevelt into reaching a decision that Root wanted him to reach and to regard as his own. The second visit was a late-night session. Root, at one point, excused himself from the room to get a document, and Roosevelt gushed: "The more I see of that man the greater he grows. Mr. Carnegie, Elihu is the wisest man I ever knew."

With that, having acted out the parts of both Roosevelt and Root as he went along, Carnegie said to his new trustees, "I beg to present him in that capacity, gentlemen, and if he will only take my advice now, I believe he will maintain his reputation."

Root's relationship with Roosevelt bore a distinct resemblance to his relationship with Carnegie. To both men, Root was a balance wheel, tempering their more extreme impulses, trying always to bring down-to-earth their more unrestrained enthusiasms. One of the most intriguing threads in the story of the Carnegie Endowment's creation was Root's conclusion, within the next year, that he could not follow the "advice" that Carnegie offered him that day.

Root's ties to Roosevelt, who was thirteen years his junior, stretched back to the beginning of Roosevelt's New York political career. When Vice President Roosevelt succeeded McKinley, Root was at his side and the first person to be consulted privately by the new president. Indeed, Root himself might have been the man to take the oath that day, had he not declined the vice presidency that Roosevelt had so reluctantly accepted. And Root was Roosevelt's first choice to be his successor in 1908. "I would walk on my hands and knees from the White House to the Capitol," Roosevelt once remarked, "to see Root made President." Roosevelt realized, however, that a man with Root's corporate-lawyer background was not electable in the Progressive Era, and Root agreed with him.

Roosevelt praised Root as the central figure in his cabinet, the man on whom he relied more than on any other and to whom he owed the most. Roosevelt once told Carnegie that Root was the greatest secretary of state in American history and the greatest cabinet officer since Alexander Hamilton. Carnegie regarded him as "a great man, and, as the greatest only are," a man "in his simplicity, sublime."

Root's decidedly stern appearance enhanced his aura of persuasiveness. One contemporary wrote that he "looks like a piece of refined steel," and "never opened his mouth without eliminating the subject under discussion." Superlatives came easily to his many admirers. Few men in public life possessed his combination of qualities: a commanding intelligence, an extraordinary knack for getting things done, a near-revered gift as a negotiator, a sardonic wit that seldom missed its mark, a finely honed aesthetic sensibility, and a personality that carried unmistakable weight and authority. All of these gave him a stature that was as formidable as it was well deserved.

Root was a brilliant administrator. The organization of America's first system for

Privately they called themselves the three musketeers. Roosevelt was Aramis. Taft was Porthos. Root was Athos.

governing overseas colonies was put in place by him, as was the structure for the modern American army and command system. His contemporaries, as well as his later biographers, differ little in their characterization of the man and his capabilities, even if they reach different judgments about his place in history.

"The personality and character of Elihu Root were not complex," one biographer has written. "In fact, he always prided himself on being direct, frank, and aboveboard. He was not, however, an easy man to know well; and any evaluation of his salient traits will vary with the degree of intimacy enjoyed by the appraiser."

A historian of the period has captured the essence of the man in a brief sketch. "Incapable of panic, loyal yet curiously detached, a constructive adviser on programs that he would not himself have initiated, Elihu Root was to his intimates, and to many who were not, the embodiment of wise and incisive judgment. He was—and the comparison is not invidious—more analytical than creative, though his organizing intelligence was perhaps the finest of his era; and his mental cast was both sharpened and narrowed by a hard-tempered realism that blunted his resentments even as it dulled his enthusiasms. . . . Lacking the moral fervor

that inspires men to supreme acts of the spirit, Root's appeal was to their instinct for order. . . . More administrator than social philosopher, he recoiled from the possible ill consequences of change as other men were attracted by its potential liberating effect. He suffered especially the conservative's dependence on convention. . . . Still, Root was never a reactionary. His brief was for a moderate, ordered, and closely controlled progress."

Three friendships mattered most to Root in his public life. His deepest personal ties and closest bonds were with Roosevelt. His years in Roosevelt's cabinets brought him into close proximity to Taft; theirs was a mutual affection that would endure for decades. His political temperament and his views of America's role in the world helped to nurture a long-standing affinity with Massachusetts Senator Henry Cabot Lodge. The agenda that Andrew Carnegie had set for his new organization and his new president of the board would soon become hostage to these three men, and Root would be caught in the crossfire.

THE OTHER TRUSTEES

Most of Carnegie's new trustees had received a simple letter in mid-November of 1910 opening with the words, "In virtue of my interest in the cause of International Peace, and in the belief that the present is an opportune time . . ." They were told that Taft and Root had already agreed to serve the board as honorary president and president. They were also told how much money was being devoted to the effort, and that its disposition would be "by such methods as the Trustees may find to be wise and feasible."

Only one of the twenty-eight men who accepted the invitation was born after the Civil War. As a collective portrait of the political and cultural establishment that dominated America during the second half of the nineteenth century, they were very nearly perfect. Patricians in the genteel tradition, they shared a fixed and certain moral credo, an unskeptical habit of mind, an undiluted faith in the possibility of social progress and in human perfectibility, and a benevolent, even redemptive, vision of America's place in the world.

They belonged to the far side of the great historical divide that Henry Steele Commager locates in the decade of the 1890s,
which for him was the watershed period in American history. "On the one side," he wrote, "lies an America predominantly agricultural; concerned with domestic problems; conforming, intellectually at least, to the political, economic, and moral principles inherited from the seventeenth and eighteenth centuries—an America still in the making, physically and socially; an America on the whole self-confident, self-contained, self-reliant, and conscious of its unique character and of a unique destiny. On the other side lies the modern America, predominantly urban and industrial; inextricably involved in world economy and politics; troubled with the problems that had long been thought peculiar to the Old World; experiencing profound changes in population, social institutions, economy, and technology; and trying to accommodate its traditional institutions and habits of thought to conditions new and in part alien."

Not less than the worlds of science, literature, and the arts were the worlds of foreign policy and diplomacy altered irreversibly by America's passage across this divide. The first generation of Endowment trustees included men who navigated this passage personally as officials in Washington, ambassadors, special negotiators, and prominent voices in the clamorous debate at the close of the century about how to fashion an American foreign policy that could be as true to still dimly perceived American interests as to fervently held American ideals. Manifest Destiny at home had, by then, been turned outward, animated by an excited and exuberant nationalism; by the economic promise of expansionism; by a peculiarly American messianic spirit; and, toward the end of the century, by a surprisingly pugnacious diplomacy.

Detached for more than a hundred years from the politics of the European powers by a historical aversion to entangling alliances, the United States had been content for decades to run a diplomacy consisting of little more than consular and commercial services, confident that its own hemisphere was a special preserve that could be protected by a Monroe Doctrine not backed up by American battleships. But at the opening of the new century the United States had come of age. As a Frenchman wrote in 1908 of this newcomer to world power, "The United States . . . . is seated at the table where the great game is played, and it cannot leave it."

John W. Foster, one of Carnegie's oldest trustees, had experienced from a special vantage point America's fitful emergence as a power to be contended with. He,

James Brown Scott   *Charles W. Eliot*   *Albert Smiley*   *Andrew Jackson Montague*   *Charlemagne Tower*

along with only a handful of other Americans, came close to being a professional diplomat. Beginning as President Ulysses S. Grant's minister to Mexico in the 1870s, he subsequently became minister to Spain and then to Russia, served briefly as secretary of state, and late in his career maintained special ties to China as an adviser and negotiator for the Manchu dynasty. Another trustee with extensive diplomatic experience was the educator Andrew D. White, first president of Cornell University, minister twice to Germany and once to Russia, and a man on whom Carnegie relied for friendship and advice. Carnegie looked often to White for his views on Germany, as he did to trustee Charlemagne Tower, who had served as chief American representative in Germany, Russia, and Austria-Hungary. And one trustee, Oscar S. Straus, had accumulated uncommon experience in the Ottoman Empire, where he represented the United States three times in as many decades.

Various members of the first board of the Endowment had accumulated important episodic experience with foreign affairs, either in Washington or abroad. A colleague and friend of Root's was lawyer Joseph H. Choate, president of the American and New York Bar associations, and late in his career ambassador to Great

Britain; it was Choate who formally accepted Carnegie's deed of trust on behalf of the board. Trustee Luke E. Wright, also a lawyer, served as ambassador to Japan and then as secretary of war in the Roosevelt years. The charter and bylaws of the new organization were prepared by trustee and lawyer John L. Cadwalader; he had done similar services for other Carnegie benefactions in the United States, and had served as assistant secretary of state earlier in his career.

Trustee James Brown Scott, who had been State Department solicitor while Root had been secretary of state, was a leading member of the community of American international lawyers deeply involved in world affairs. As a condition for his own willingness to serve as president of the Endowment's board, Root insisted that Scott become both the full-time executive officer of the organization in Washington and secretary of the board. And trustee Andrew Jackson Montague, former governor of Virginia, had garnered, like other politicians of stature, a smattering of exposure to diplomacy. One of the youngest men on the board, he had been appointed by Secretary of State Root to delegations at international conferences, had achieved recognition as a progressive Democratic spokesman for the New

South, and was asked by Root to join the organizing committee for the new Endowment.

Other men of national reputation to whom Carnegie turned when selecting his board had established special niches for themselves in the American policy discourse during these years, even if they had never held diplomatic positions. Foremost in this category was trustee Charles W. Eliot. "President Eliot," as he was known by a generation of Americans, had led Harvard University for forty years before his retirement in 1909. Eliot, perhaps more purely than any other member of the Endowment board, embodied a nineteenth-century spirit, bringing to international affairs the same reformist instincts, the same unbridled confidence and attachment to universal values that he brought to a life of university building and leadership in American culture. Trustee Albert K. Smiley had become host to an establishment newly interested in foreign affairs and willing in greater numbers, and with increasing frequency, to attend the conferences that Smiley sponsored at his famous Lake Mohonk resort center in upstate New York.

Sharing with Root a place in the Endowment's inner circle was trustee Nicholas Murray Butler. President of Columbia Uni-

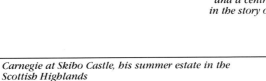

Carnegie at Skibo Castle, his summer estate in the
Scottish Highlands

versity and an active internationalist, Butler, like White, was one of Carnegie's "Old Shoes"—a special term of endearment reserved for those whom he regularly invited to his vast summer estate and residence in Scotland, Skibo Castle. (If heaven is much different from Skibo, the laird of the manor told friends, then somebody made a very great mistake.) Carnegie felt close personal affection and respect for Butler, even though Root always remained primus inter pares, and

even though Butler's baroque personality stood in such sharp contrast to Carnegie's own simple and direct style. Butler's flamboyance invited caricature. Striving and ambitious and enamored of pomp, he cut a figure more regal than royalty. He traveled and entertained on a grand scale. He cultivated the great and near-great and opened his autobiography in later years with a long recitation of how many of them he had known and how well. He was an imposing orator, a tireless corre-

spondent, and a relentless promoter of the ideas and institutions identified with his name. He was involved in many worlds: in Republican party politics, in education, in domestic politics, and in international affairs. During the years of discussions and maneuvering leading up to the establishment of the Endowment, no one was more intimately involved from more angles than Butler.

11

"Taftism"—peace through arbitration

A presidential speech . . .

A Presidential Peace Policy

The presidency of William Howard Taft was a historical parenthesis separating the Roosevelt and Wilson eras. Taft was a mystery to no one. Genial, timid, conventional, somehow spongy in character, this huge hulk of a man lacked passion as well as ambition, though he did show flashes of solid good humor. More often than was prudent, Taft admitted his distaste for politics, his dislike of the controversies bred by politics, and his discomfort with the excitable public he never quite seemed to understand. Roosevelt pumped up Taft's political career at every turn, and in the beginning their friendship was affectionate and genuine. Roosevelt nudged and tutored Taft into the presidency that Mrs. Taft wanted for her husband more than he did himself. Yet Roosevelt, in the end, wreaked havoc on Taft and his administration. By 1912 their embittered personal relations and fierce policy clashes had left the Republican party in shambles and produced one of the most tempestuous personal rifts in American political history.

TAFT SPEAKS

"Being a lawyer," the progressive journalist William Allen White once wrote of Taft, "he trusted . . . the spur of the moment to inspire him when he spoke; this partly because he was indifferent to what he said, not remotely realizing the import of the spoken words of a President to a multitude; and again, partly because he would prefer to talk to his friends, take his ease, and do some other task rather than prepare a speech. He had no sense of the importance of a speech as a speech, nor of any other public contact as part of a statesman's job."

Taft delivered just such a speech at the Hotel Astor in New York City on March 22, 1910. He was the guest of honor at a banquet attended by a large, blue-ribbon audience whose members were for the most part strong boosters of military preparedness. Taft gave them what they had come to hear, a promise to keep building battleships, an assurance that peace through strength was indispensable in the short term. And he gave them something else, a little discourse on the virtues of peace through arbitration. This was the first step toward what would become one of the most divisive episodes of Taft's presidency, although neither he nor his listeners realized it that evening.

"I have noticed exceptions in our arbitration treaties," Taft observed matter-of-factly, "as to reference of questions of honor, of national honor, to courts of arbitration. Personally, I don't see any more reason why matters of national honor should not be referred to a court of arbitration." He continued in a meandering understatement. "I know that is going further than most men are willing to go, but as among men, we have to submit differences even if they involve honor, now, if we obey the law, to the court, or let them go undecided. It is true that our courts can enforce the law, and as between nations there is no court with a sheriff or a marshal that can enforce the law. But I do not see why questions of honor may not be submitted to a tribunal supposed to be composed of men of honor who understand questions of national honor, to abide by their decision, as well as any other question of difference arising between nations."

Only Taft could have ended with: "And, now, ladies and gentlemen, I have done. I did not expect to talk quite so long . . . and if what I have said seems to lack preparation, you may understand that you cannot

... convinced Carnegie to strike his bargain with Taft. The president would promote arbitration. Carnegie would set up a peace endowment to support his policy.

prepare every speech, however dignified and however attractive the audience."

CARNEGIE REACTS

This was the speech that fired Carnegie into action in the early months of 1910 and led, as much as any other event, to the creation of the Carnegie Endowment. And it did much more. Casually though it was enunciated—Taft later admitted this, saying that its pro-arbitration sentiment had been intended in part to defuse criticism of his continuing support for naval preparedness—it was a speech that brought to a head the first great confrontation between nationalist and internationalist impulses in modern American foreign policy. Few people now remember this confrontation. But during the last two years of the Taft administration it was a cause célèbre, an acute and at times virulent clash that plagued the amiable man in the White House.

The speech led to a Taft peace policy that the president eventually came to regard as "the great jewel of my administration. . . . the greatest act during these four years." It produced the foreign-policy issue that precipitated the final break between Roosevelt and Taft. It brought into collision the philosophies of peace through strength and peace through arbitration. It pitted the president against the

Senate and against Lodge, then chairman of the Foreign Relations Committee. It gave the senator an opportunity to provide an eerie preview of the strategy he would adopt at the end of the decade against Woodrow Wilson's campaign to bring the United States into the League of Nations.

As a putative solution to the problem of international war, the notion of "arbitration" sounds to our modern ear faintly archaic and musty, a legalistic, ever-so-polite remedy long discredited by twentieth-century history and by its wars, which have proved power, not law, to be the real arbiter among nations. But to those sitting in Taft's audience the word had an immediate resonance, laden with emotive power and political symbolism. To know what a person thought about arbitration—for it, against it, for it conditionally, against it conditionally, for it in these specific circumstances, against it in those—to know these things when Taft was president was to know something important about what that person believed America should stand for in the world.

In the century since arbitral provisions

had been incorporated into a treaty signed by John Jay with the British in 1794, nations had come to accept as fairly routine the notion that they could resort to arbitration when it suited their interests. Although the details varied from case to case, procedures usually required disputing nations to appoint their own arbitrators to a special panel, supplemented, if necessary, by other panel members selected by agreed-upon third parties. Decisions were to be reached on the basis of accepted legal norms and principles. More judicial in character than other techniques of dispute settlement in the international repertory, such as mediation and regular diplomatic negotiations, arbitration had become for Great Britain and the United States a frequently used device for dealing with a variety of problems. The informed public in both countries had developed more than a passing familiarity with the arbitration idea, while legal professionals had already studied thoroughly the accumulated practice.

Every major period in the history of American foreign policy seems to cast up certain compressed ideas or concepts that

THE ALABAMA CLAIMS.

Probability of a Satisfactory Ending
of the Controversy.

The Latest Aspect of the Question in England.

No Official News Received by the United
States Government.

The arbitration movement
began with the Alabama
controversy just after the
Civil War.

The British saw a greedy
Uncle Sam inflating
American claims.

become code words and litmus tests for arguments about American power and purpose. The generation of Americans that took its cues from George Washington's Farewell Address argued about "entangling alliances." The generation that lived with the years of indecision between World War I and World War II argued about "isolation." And a nuclear age generation has argued about "détente." So, too, at the turn of the century, did Americans rail against the dangers of arbitration or embrace its promise; endorse it as a vehicle for spreading influence and values worldwide or condemn it as a path toward weakness and submission; equate it with responsible internationalism or dismiss it as a naive illusion.

Taft knew all of this. He knew that arbitration was controversial. His involvement with the arbitration movement had begun long before he entered the White House. What Taft did not know was that by voicing a more unqualified commitment to arbitration than any president before him had done, he was setting in motion a chain of events that would give the arbitration movement and its friends not only more visibility than at any time in its forty-year history, but also more vulnerability to their opponents.

THE ARBITRATION MOVEMENT

Carnegie had been lukewarm about Taft during the 1908 election campaign, thinking him markedly less attractive than the New York reform governor Charles Evans Hughes as a Republican opponent against William Jennings Bryan. For Carnegie, Taft was too much the uncritical representative of the most conservative elements in the Roosevelt administration, in which he had lately served as secretary of war, succeeding Root.

But when Carnegie read Taft's arbitration speech while vacationing at the Grand Canyon, he underwent instant and total conversion. A jubilant Carnegie immediately dashed off a laudatory letter to Taft urging him to remain true to the promise of his speech. "No words from any Ruler of our time, or indeed of any of the past, so heavily laden with precious fruit," Carnegie wrote, "not for our nation only, but for mankind, as those you have just spoken in New York." Carnegie also went quickly into public print. He expanded the letter into an article in the *Century Magazine,* outlining the problems of strengthening arbitration and declaring that "the solution came unexpectedly in a flash of inspiration from no less a ruler

than President Taft." Carnegie sent Roosevelt a draft of the article before publication, and urged him to support Taft's arbitration policy. Carnegie, for the next two years, devoted little attention to any other public issue. He felt that the arbitration movement was finally on the verge of a real breakthrough after more than three decades of desultory growth.

In the post-Civil War 1880s Americans remembered the *Alabama* as they were later to "Remember the *Maine*" in the patriotic rallying cry of the Spanish-American War. No Confederate raiding ship was more famous in the South or more notorious in the North than the *Alabama.* Outfitted in England and equipped with English guns, crewmen, and supplies, the *Alabama* had slipped out of the country under the noses of ostensibly neutral English officials and gone on to destroy Union ships. The vessel became for Americans the symbol of British opposition to Abraham Lincoln's aims during the Civil War. Against the background of the American

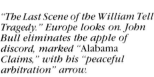

"The Last Scene of the William Tell Tragedy." Europe looks on. John Bull eliminates the apple of discord, marked "Alabama Claims," with his "peaceful arbitration" arrow.

Albert J. Beveridge, Anglo-Saxonism incarnate

Revolution and the War of 1812, Anglo-American relations remained troubled and uncertain during the second half of the nineteenth century. When the rapprochement finally came during the years leading up to World War I, it fundamentally changed the geopolitics of American foreign policy.

But the rapprochement did not come easily. It began with the successful resolution of claims arising from the *Alabama's* wartime depredations. Absent a settlement, some distinguished American politicians threatened to seize Canada from Britain as compensation. England first insisted that the *Alabama* case could never be subjected to international arbitration because it involved matters of national honor. The settlement was reached when Great Britain, eager to patch up its relations with the United States because of more pressing priorities in Europe, agreed to arbitrate the issue in a treaty that included an apology by the British for letting the *Alabama* "escape" and a set of rules of neutrality for the arbitral commission to use in its judgment. In 1872, the commission awarded the United States $15.5 million in damages. British officials later hung the canceled check on a wall at

the Foreign Office as an antiarbitration warning to future diplomats. Carnegie, however, saw only the brighter side. England and America, he later said, had "taught the world Arbitration."

ANGLO-SAXONISM

The arbitration movement was rooted in a quintessentially nineteenth-century amalgam of ideas and sentiments, all of them reaching well beyond the technicalities of international law. An essential ingredient was the mystique of Anglo-Saxonism. The elites and intelligentsia on both sides of the Atlantic spoke unselfconsciously during the reign of Darwin about "patriotism of race," or a "race alliance," or "race imperialism." These terms were associated with notions that were at one extreme pacific and humanitarian, and at the other, belligerent and acquisitive.

One of Carnegie's ideological heroes, the British Quaker and Chartist leader John Bright, wrote in the 1880s: "England and [the] United States are two nations, but I always like to regard them as one people. On them the growth of all that is good in the world greatly depends."

"Race," Carnegie wrote at the end of the

century, "is the potent factor," and it has been said that he "perhaps best expressed the racial rhetoric that provided much of the intellectual cement for Anglo-American understanding."

Theodore Roosevelt, whose early and typical Yankee Anglophobia softened as he matured, wrote before the end of the century, "I think the twentieth century will still be the century of the men who speak English." Another enthusiast for Anglo-Saxon destiny voiced confidence that "the Anglo-Saxon race assimilates and is never itself assimilated. It is the dominant element; it comes to the top; it rules." Rudyard Kipling's poems "The White Man's Burden" and "Gunga Din" best expressed a romanticized version of imperial obligation. The arch-imperialist Senator Albert J. Beveridge, who accepted an interpretation of history that traced Anglo-Saxon roots back to ancient Teutonic democracy, extolled another version of the imperial future, one having a ring of pure zealotry. "God has not been preparing the English-speaking and Teutonic peoples for a thousand years for nothing but vain and idle self-admiration," he thundered during a Senate debate. "No! He has made us the master organizers of the world to establish system where chaos reigns...."

All is well since all grows better

Andrew Carnegie

Feb 12th 1973.

English social philosopher Herbert Spencer inspired Carnegie's optimistic motto, "All is well since all grows better."

SOCIAL DARWINISM

Naturally, the proponents of arbitration identified themselves with the more benevolent strains of Anglo-Saxonism, and to these they added a second ingredient from the nineteenth-century amalgam: the optimistic evolutionary vision of Herbert Spencer's Social Darwinism. It is almost impossible to overstate the impact that this great English philosopher had on American life and thought after the Civil War. For highbrow and lowbrow circles alike, he was the prophet of the age, the "metaphysician of the homemade intellectual," as he was described by Richard Hofstadter. His ponderous theories applied evolutionary principles from the biological sciences to the development of society. His doctrines of inevitable progress, with their patina of scientific proof and their easy conversion into simple maxims and slogans, captured the imagination of a public eager for the message.

To believe, as most arbitration adherents did, that a permanent Anglo-American arbitration treaty was a first step toward the creation of an ever-widening circle of countries who would agree to settle their disputes by judicial means, was to adopt a perfectly Spencerian view of how international society would develop. And to believe that the English-speaking core for this peaceful world was destined to leadership by its cultural superiority was to give Anglo-Saxonism its natural, historically ordained place in the evolving scheme.

Andrew Carnegie and Herbert Spencer were devoted friends. Although different in their temperaments and intellectual styles, they enjoyed an extended and intense personal relationship, and their correspondence vividly illuminates the personality of the mercurial and cranky philosopher during his final years. Few moments in Carnegie's life were as important to him as those witnessed by a throng of reporters at a dock side in New York in the autumn of 1882. Spencer had just completed his celebrated pilgrimage to the United States, orchestrated and stage-managed in part by Carnegie. While awaiting the departure of his steamship, Spencer suddenly grabbed the hands of two men who had come to see him off. One was Edward Youmans, a magazine editor who was Spencer's greatest popularizer in this country. The other was Carnegie. "Here," he proclaimed, "are my two best American friends."

Many years later Carnegie recalled in his autobiography that his own lifelong motto, "All is well since all grows better," was inspired by Spencer, for whom progress was "not an accident, but a necessity." And Carnegie shared with his great teacher a deep aversion to war, militarism, and imperialism. For both men, America's colonial acquisition of the Philippines and England's war with the Boers in South Africa stood as examples of the misguided follies that did no credit to the two branches of the Anglo-Saxon race in which they placed their faith.

Although Carnegie's substantive grasp of Spencer's formidable theories was shaky, he never doubted the philosopher's hopeful and promising vision of the future. Never did Carnegie's enthusiasm for arbitration lose its Spencerian ring. He remained confident that arbitration was more than merely a short-term fix for international problems. He saw it as the critical core for an evolutionary process that would inexorably work its way toward a peaceful world, a world in which civilization would finally triumph over barbarism. By referring as often as he did to an expectation that one day nations would forgo war just as civilized societies

THE AMERICANISATION OF THE WORLD

By W. T. STEAD.

1/-

Belief in arbitration meant belief in America, typified by this British book.

SECRETARY OF STATE
U.S. SENATOR

JURISPRUDENCE

INTERNATIONAL LAW

BLACKSTONE

Root and other international lawyers identified arbitration with belief in law.

"What arbitration would mean." Critics warned that arbitration would weaken America. Here, John Bull disarms Uncle Sam, slipping the six-shooter from his pocket.

had already forgone cannibalism and dueling, Carnegie was not using an idle figure of speech. He was, rather, relying upon the common parlance of like-minded Spencerians of his day.

FAITH IN LAW

The nineteenth-century amalgam of ideas that nourished the arbitration movement blended a third ingredient with Anglo-Saxonism and Spencerian optimism: a nearly unadulterated faith in law and legal procedures. As de Tocqueville and many other observers of the American scene appreciated, Americans respected their laws, venerated their Constitution, and sanctified their judicial procedures. Americans believed that their national legal system was a beacon for an international legal order. They believed, as Root once said when characterizing federal practice as a model for international arbitration, that "the whole world owes too much to the

Constitution of the United States to think little of its example."

Americans, especially their largely lawyer-dominated establishment, appeared convinced that international peace and international law were handmaidens, just as were domestic tranquility and national law in the American national experience. Americans could place this much faith in the global relevance of law because foreign affairs, for them, had been a fairly uncomplicated experience so far. International frictions for Americans had grown not out of the great power struggles and ideological clashes that would later dominate the twentieth century, but rather out of myriad disputes over boundaries, collection of foreign debts, protection of citizens abroad, rights on the high seas, and interpretations of existing international legal instruments. Judicial techniques for dealing with such matters seemed just, practical, and obvious.

This American faith in law was not selfless. It rested, for many arbitration proponents, on an often unstated premise that the United States in its international behavior would always be on the right side of the law, that arbitration would always promote American interests, and that the United States would always be vindicated if challenged to an arbitral contest by other countries. "I believe in arbitration," a speaker at one of Albert Smiley's Mohonk conferences proclaimed, "because I believe in the American people." Internationalism through arbitration would not sacrifice American national objectives. It was nothing less than Americanism writ large in the world arena, an internationalism of high purpose, low risk, and good feeling. Not for the last time in the twentieth century did Americans wrap their internationalism in nationalist garb, professing to believe that the tensions were not serious between their national instincts and their internationalist ideals.

President Grover Cleveland plunged America and England into a crisis over Venezuela.

THE ANGLO-AMERICAN CRISIS OVER VENEZUELA

These tensions surfaced often after the *Alabama* settlement, as it became evident that arbitration, underneath the gilding and gloss of the reformers, was a diplomatic weapon. It was an adjunct to power politics rather than a substitute for it. It enabled the powerful to dictate to the powerless under the guise of lawfulness. Or it could provide a defensive shield for a weaker state against a stronger one unwilling to use force to work its will. Seen in these terms, arbitration's virtues and vices were judged on grounds of expediency as well as ideology. Favor it when it works for you; oppose it when it does not.

In 1895, arbitration was used as a headline-grabbing instrument of American diplomacy. Grover Cleveland's Democratic administration twisted the British lion's tail violently and pushed America and England onto a collision course during a now-forgotten controversy between Venezuela and Great Britain. The real issue was American fear of British penetration into the Caribbean in disregard of the Monroe Doctrine. The diplomatic imbroglio turned on whether Britain would arbitrate the dispute with Venezuela, as the United States demanded.

London and Caracas had long disagreed about the precise location of the boundary between British Guiana and Venezuela. By the middle of the 1890s the discovery of gold in the border hinterlands had turned a backwater dispute into a major international controversy. Previously Venezuela had attempted unsuccessfully to persuade Britain to arbitrate the dispute and then to convince the United States to encourage arbitration under the principles of the Monroe Doctrine. Britain was by far the dominant force in the disputed border area and resolutely refused to arbitrate away its stronger position. Venezuela had wanted the United States or Spain to arbitrate, thinking that either country would be biased against British claims, which was exactly the fear of the Foreign Office in London. And, more than that, the British wanted to avoid an adverse precedent. London did not want other disputes in its colonial areas to be inflated by troublemakers who would then demand arbitration that

would work against British interests.

The controversy remained at an impasse until personal conviction and politics conspired to push the normally cautious and peace-minded Cleveland into a more confrontational posture toward Britain. He was not sympathetic to Britain's position in the dispute. His Republican opponents tagged him with running a weak foreign policy. Accusations that he was pro-British were a severe political liability among electorally important Irish-American voters. Moreover, he had not taken a strong stand against other recent British meddling in Latin America. And Congress was now urging that England submit to arbitration.

Cleveland's heavy-handed and aggressive secretary of state, Richard Olney, accelerated the drift toward confrontation by sending Britain an extraordinary demand in the summer of 1895. The United States was "practically sovereign" in the Western Hemisphere, Olney wrote in a celebrated diplomatic note. The United States was entitled to intervene between Britain and Venezuela on the basis of the Monroe Doctrine. Britain must arbitrate the dispute in full. If it refused, the president would turn the whole question over to Congress—implying activation of the power to declare war. Even Carnegie,

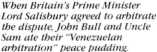

When Britain's Prime Minister Lord Salisbury agreed to arbitrate the dispute, John Bull and Uncle Sam ate their "Venezuelan arbitration" peace pudding.

though torn between patriotism for his adopted country and residual sympathy for Great Britain, placed himself squarely in the "arbitrate-or-else" camp, where he was allied with Lodge and others eager to face down the British.

Leading Britain at the time was the brilliant and experienced Lord Salisbury, one of the ablest statesmen of the day. He did not yet take seriously America's pretensions to regional hegemony, much less to world power, and he treated the warlike noises from Washington as empty bluster. He waited four months before responding to Cleveland, and then he was blunt. The Monroe Doctrine had nothing to do with the case, and Britain would not arbitrate under any circumstances.

Cleveland then delivered an end-of-year message to Congress that was stunningly bellicose. The United States would appoint its own commission to determine the boundary, Congress was told, and any refusal by Britain to abide by the findings would constitute willful aggression upon the United States. The meaning was clear, and even the circumspect Salisbury acknowledged the chance that "war with the United States is a distinct possibility in the not distant future."

Salisbury's good sense, as well as events in another corner of the world, defused

the crisis in a matter of weeks. Britain was edging toward war with the Boers in South Africa, and in early January 1896, armed British raiders penetrated the Boer Transvaal Republic. They were soundly repulsed, and Kaiser Wilhelm II dispatched a notorious telegram congratulating the leader of the Boers on his success. It was as clumsy and ill-considered a piece of diplomacy as Olney's and Cleveland's, but it mattered much more. It became, for an outraged British public, a major incident in the deterioration of Anglo-German relations.

The affair pushed the United States and England further toward their historic rapprochement. Britain a few years later supported America in its war with Spain and thereafter gave far greater credence to America's status as a potential world power. Salisbury calculated that England's intensifying rivalry with Germany placed a high premium on assuring America's friendship for strategic reasons, quite apart from its cultural imperatives. In his *Education,* Henry Adams characterized "the sudden appearance of Germany as the grizzly terror which in twenty years effected what Adamses had tried for two hundred in vain—frightened England into America's arms."

THE OLNEY-PAUNCEFOTE TREATY

By mid-January 1896, Salisbury had backed off from his blanket rejection of the American démarche, opening the door to secret negotiations between London and Washington. Before these were concluded, the British government set aside its antiarbitration reservations and came up with a tactic intended to distract American attention from Venezuela and to serve as extra insurance against American enmity in future crises. Britain offered the United States a general treaty of arbitration covering most categories of possible disputes. This step must have made Salisbury swallow very hard indeed, for he once remarked that "like competitive examinations and sewage irrigation, arbitration is one of the famous nostrums of the age. Like them it will have its day and will pass away, and future ages will look with pity and contempt on those who could have believed in such an expedient for bridling the ferocity of human passions."

The treaty was signed in January 1897 by Olney and the British ambassador in Washington, Sir Julian Pauncefote. McKinley, Cleveland's successor, strongly endorsed this unprecedented document in his inaugural address and urged the Senate to ratify it.

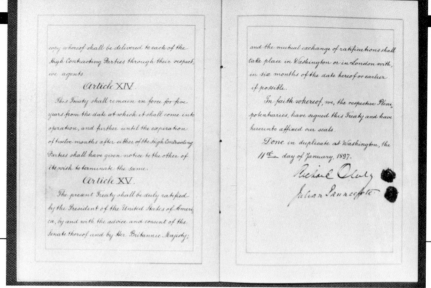

ARBITRATION ASSURED

The General Treaty Between the United States and Great Britain Is Signed and Sent to the Senate.

TEXT OF PRESIDENT CLEVELAND'S MESSAGE OF TRANSMITTAL.

Washington and London then signed a far-reaching arbitration treaty covering future disputes. Known as the Olney-Pauncefote Treaty, the pact was defeated by the Senate.

The Olney-Pauncefote Treaty was a milestone in the surge of the arbitration movement late in the century, even though it was defeated in the Senate by three votes. The defeat came after the treaty had been amended beyond recognition by legislators still harboring pervasive anti-British sentiments, reluctant to constrain future American efforts to limit European influence in the Western Hemisphere, and determined not to compromise a number of American economic interests. Public support for the treaty was thin, though vocal, despite the administration's campaign to drum up enthusiasm among leading sectors of public opinion. The Senate, not yet a popularly elected body, prevailed easily.

Nevertheless, by demonstrating that general arbitration might have a political future in more favorable circumstances, the Olney-Pauncefote Treaty galvanized the proarbitrationists. Most important, it solidified their natural bond with promoters of Anglo-American understanding, who regarded the treaty as "one of the greatest events of modern history." The treaty also signaled the onset of a shift in the American peace movement. It moved away from the absolute pacifism and moralism of earlier decades, and toward a more establishment, mainstream, and even conservative core, dominated by the professional and business classes that by the early twentieth century had become the mainstay of the arbitration movement. By that time, as John Dos Passos would write many years later, "arbitration had been in the air for a decade."

The Olney-Paucefote Treaty, predictably, invigorated nationalistic opponents of arbitration as well. They sharpened their claims that Americans could not have general arbitration and still have the protective tariffs that they so desperately wanted, or the canal across Central America, or the privileged access to disputed territories and oceanic fishing grounds—and so on—with appeals to a variety of special interests that could possibly be disadvantaged by an arbitration regime. In sum, the treaty brought general arbitration out of the realm of virtuous ideals and into the arenas of international realpolitik, domestic political controversy, and chronic senatorial resistance to any encroachment on its own treaty-making prerogatives.

THE CARNEGIE ENDOWMENT PRINCIPALS AND ARBITRATION DIPLOMACY

For Andrew Carnegie the Olney-Pauncefote Treaty symbolized the unfinished business on the arbitration agenda. His deed of trust for the Carnegie Endowment stated that the new peace policy announced by President Taft was an opportunity to pick up where the treaty had left off thirteen years earlier. What Carnegie's new trustees thought of his assertion in the deed that Taft's policy "seems within easy reach of success" is a matter for speculation. What is certain, however, is that the dozen or so of them who had had significant foreign-policy experience were as well positioned as any men of their generation to appreciate both the promise and the pitfalls of arbitration. For the single most distinctive common feature of their public careers was their link to arbitration diplomacy and to the arbitration movement, both before and after the Venezuela episode.

Delegates to the Hague Conference of 1899 reached an international agreement on arbitration.

ARBITRATION AND ANDREW CARNEGIE

Most of these new trustees presumably knew how far back Carnegie's own involvement with arbitration stretched. In the 1880s he had been engaged in the first approach to America by British advocates of a general bilateral arbitration agreement. A leader of the British labor movement, Randal Cremer, founder of the International Arbitration League in 1871, had got his colleagues in the House of Commons to pledge their support for a treaty so that the proposal could be discussed with the president of the United States. Acting as Cremer's interlocutor in the United States, Carnegie arranged for Cleveland to receive a visiting British delegation headed by Cremer in 1887. Cleveland was cautious and promised nothing. He knew that Senate opposition was strong to pending treaties with Great Britain, and he anticipated that with an approaching national election, open sympathy for Cremer's proposal would provoke the usual anti-British sentiments from Irish-Americans.

Cremer's delegation, moreover, experienced firsthand the fury of Irish-American passions during public meetings disrupted by shouts of "Remember the *Alabama!*" "Home Rule for Ireland!" "Give us arbitration for Ireland!" and "We want no peace with England!" Although Cremer and American supporters of arbitration made modest progress in stimulating congressional and public interest, the momentum soon flagged. Carnegie then joined those who, at the beginning of the 1890s, sought to develop an arbitration regime to govern U.S. relations with Latin America.

Carnegie's friend James Blaine was secretary of state under Republican president Benjamin Harrison, whose administration was in power between Cleveland's first and second terms. Blaine persuaded Harrison to appoint Carnegie an official delegate to the first Pan-American Congress in 1889-1890—his first and only service as an official of the U.S. government. Blaine's goals in Latin America were simple. He wanted to keep regional peace in order to avoid European intervention, and to enlarge American trade and commercial relations with the region. Both premises served as operational guides for American policy around the turn of the century. Blaine believed that a multilateral arbitration accord for the hemisphere would further Washington's objectives, and he got the Pan-American Congress to endorse a draft treaty. But this program, too, faltered rapidly when the United States and Chile became embroiled in a feud before the treaty was sent to the Senate. The administration then decided that arbitration might not be a very good idea after all if it limited U.S. responses to such problems. The Latin Americans also had second thoughts, suspecting that Washington might one day engineer disputes as a pretext for activating arbitration against weaker states in the hemisphere. Letting the multilateral draft pass quietly from the diplomatic scene seemed best to all concerned.

ARBITRATION AND KEY TRUSTEES

Among Carnegie trustees experienced in arbitration diplomacy, John Foster occupied a place of special and early prominence. Immediately after resigning as secretary of state in the early 1880s, he led the American team in one of the most important arbitrations of the decade, over contending British and American claims to sealing rights in the Bering Sea. That the decision went against the United States did not deflect Foster from what would become a lifelong conviction that arbitration should be an important component in responsible American diplomacy.

Andrew White, while ambassador to Germany, played a pivotal role as head of the American delegation in the first international diplomatic effort to achieve a multilateral arbitration agreement, the

21

One U.S. delegate at The Hague was Alfred Thayer Mahan, America's premier theorist of sea power and a persistent critic of arbitration.

Roosevelt's views on arbitration were to complicate the story of the Carnegie Endowment. As "The World's Constable" he wielded an arbitration treaty and his big stick.

Critics said Roosevelt's ambition was to exchange his Roughrider's hat for a European imperial crown.

Roosevelt negotiated bilateral arbitration treaties in 1904. Here, the Senate's "Brutus" Lodge, his dagger marked "arbitration treaties," attacks "Caesar" Roosevelt.

Hague Conference of 1899. Czar Nicholas II's surprise call for the conference had little to do with peace or, originally, with arbitration. Increasingly worried by the accelerating pace of the armaments build-up in Europe, the Russian leader wanted a disarmament agreement so that the financial and technical burdens of his competition with the Germans and the French could be eased. Western distrust of the czar's motives was limitless, and practical prospects for an arms limitation agreement were virtually nil. Knowing this, proponents of arbitration stepped into the breach and succeeded in widening the agenda to include one of their favorite ideas for "perfecting" the essentially ad hoc practice of arbitration; they urged the creation of a permanent tribunal.

White was sympathetic, though pragmatic enough to turn aside the more off-beat suggestions from peace activists with pet schemes for The Hague. He was a believer in progress toward a better arbitration regime, and he had the support of both President McKinley and Secretary of State John Hay. White, in fact, hoped that improvements in arbitration procedures might even open the door to arms limitation—arbitration before disarmament, he would say. He was able to persuade a reluctant Germany to be flexible in the

Hague negotiations, in part because his ambitions were modest. "As to arbitration," he wrote in his diary, "we cannot make it compulsory, as so many very good people wish; it is clear that no power here would agree to that; but even to provide regular machinery for arbitration, constantly in the sight of all nations, and always ready for use, would be a great gain." The outcome at The Hague was meager. A permanent court of arbitration was established, its name grander than its reality. It was actually little more than a standing panel of arbiters who could be called into service by disputing nations willing to rely on arbitration.

Another Carnegie trustee and the Endowment's first vice president, Joseph Choate, played a key part in the next American effort to improve multilateral arbitration, at the second Hague Conference in 1907. President Roosevelt masterminded Washington's strategy, Secretary Root coordinated it, and Choate executed it. Neither Choate nor Root could have known it at the time, but Roosevelt's views on arbitration were to have a dramatic impact on their peace endowment a few years hence. By 1907 those views had taken shape and been voiced with some clarity.

Roosevelt was ambivalent about arbitration. He was skeptical, even contemptu-

ous, about it as a general remedy for the ills of an increasingly fractious international society, or as a substitute for war among nations. He was measured, although occasionally enthusiastic, about it as a lever in the big-stick diplomacy he relished, so long as it did not risk American interests or imply American unwillingness to use force to back up its objectives. When the United States lost the Bering Sea arbitrations Roosevelt complained to his friend Lodge that the episode represented a foreign-policy failure. Overeagerness to reach a peaceful settlement, he thought, had opened the way to more compromise than was prudent. "It should teach us," he said, "to be exceedingly cautious about entering into any arbitration." When debate later raged about the Olney-Pauncefote Treaty, he was candid. "I believe in arbitration and in peace," he proclaimed, "but we would dearly purchase a hundred arbitration treaties if they lulled us into trusting to them alone to preserve peace . . . I hope we will ratify the treaty and build ten new battleships."

Roosevelt must have been reassured by the fact that his confidant, Admiral Alfred Thayer Mahan, the ultranationalist theorist of American sea power and glorifier of the military virtues so admired by Roosevelt, was a member of the U.S. delegation at the

SENATE BREAKS WITH PRESIDENT

---

50 to 9 It Spurns His Advice on Arbitration.

first Hague Conference, and thus able to restrain any excessive enthusiasms by the arbitrationists. Soon after becoming president, however, Roosevelt himself stimulated some international recourse to the new Hague arbitration machinery. Having by then toned down his belligerent earlier rhetoric, he sensed more keenly than most American leaders that a general war in Europe or Asia would harm American interests. He thought a prudent peace diplomacy was essential. Arbitration could help here and there, even if it could not produce miracles.

Having instructed his first secretary of state, the aging John Hay, to settle a long-standing minor dispute with Mexico through the Hague Court—its first case—Roosevelt wanted this example to encourage other powers to make modest use of the court. They did so during the next decade. Then Roosevelt exerted very considerable pressure, mainly on Germany but also on England and Italy, to resolve through the Hague Court their serious collective dispute with Venezuela during a 1902 crisis over an outstanding debt. Always, however, the Rooseveltian touch was there: "Important though it is that we should get the Hague Tribunal to act in this case, where it can properly act," he observed, "it is very much more impor-

tant that we have a first-class navy and an efficient, though small army. No Hague Court will save us if we come short in these respects."

Roosevelt's extreme caution about exposing important American interests to possibly adverse arbitral decisions was particularly obvious during a set-to with Great Britain in his first administration. Canada had made extravagant and unsustainable claims to contested boundary areas in Alaska, newly important because of the discovery of possible gold deposits. At the urging of Canada, Britain tried to get Roosevelt to arbitrate the dispute according to normal methods. London predictably argued that Britain had done so when the roles were reversed in the Venezuela crisis. Roosevelt said no—and reminded Britain that it resolutely resisted efforts to subject its conflict with the Boers to arbitration. The Canadian claims, he said, were a sham. For the United States to give them legitimacy, he was convinced, would simply open the door to other spurious claims against the United States.

A new mix of muscle flexing and diplomacy was needed, Roosevelt decided. He instructed his secretary of war, Elihu Root, to move troops quietly into southern Alaska. Then Roosevelt, while making clear his absolute unwillingness to compromise

the basic position he had taken all along, agreed to an arbitration arrangement transparently loaded in Washington's favor. After face-saving maneuvers by all concerned, the issue was resolved in a settlement that essentially satisfied Roosevelt's terms without doing severe damage to Washington's relations with London. The last major territorial dispute blocking Anglo-American rapprochement was now out of the way.

During his first term, Roosevelt had also had a taste of how difficult it could be to maneuver even limited arbitration treaties through a Senate jealous of its prerogatives and beholden to political interests opposed to arbitration. Roosevelt had endorsed arbitration in his 1903 annual message to Congress and had encouraged Hay to negotiate with ten countries a cluster of arbitration treaties, all of them conditional and fully protective of national sovereignty and honor, and modeled on a recent British-French treaty.

When the Senate amended the treaties into empty shells in 1905, Roosevelt was furious but powerless to counter the Senate. So he simply refused to accept the Senate's version, despite the urgings of arbitration proponents who believed he should do so. "Such is the opinion of all of us who have labored for these treaties

"The Call of the Wild." Having selectively favored arbitration, Roosevelt was petitioned from many quarters.

During the Roosevelt years, members of the establishment met annually at the Lake Mohonk Conferences on International Arbitration in upstate New York. At far right, the 1905 conference. Mohonk was the idyllic summer residence of Albert Smiley, later an Endowment trustee.

from Ex Sec'y Foster down—No one in half a million will ever note the amendments," Carnegie told the president. Subsequently, when the time came to plan for the second Hague Conference, Roosevelt decided, on Root's advice, to adjust his proposal for a multilateral arbitration agreement to take account of the main thrust of the senatorial objections to his bilateral treaties; in effect, he gave the Senate a veto over any specific presidential decision to arbitrate, even under the terms of a general treaty accepted by the United States.

By the time the president and now Secretary of State Root had to formulate for Choate a set of negotiating guidelines for the 1907 Hague meeting, Roosevelt had come to "fear quite as much the amiable but irrational enthusiasts for an impossible progress in peace as I do those who desire that no real progress shall be made in the matter." He confided privately to British Foreign Secretary Sir Edward Grey: "Personally I think that the strengthening of the Hague Court is of more consequence than disarmament. Every effort should be made to extend the number of

possible international disputes which are to be subjected to arbitration, and above all to make it easier to secure effective arbitration." Reflecting his unhappiness with the earlier senatorial resistance that now required modification of the treaty proposal for The Hague, however, Roosevelt explained to Grey that "it does not represent any real advance for me or anyone else to sign a general arbitration treaty which itself merely expresses a 'pious opinion' that there ought hereafter to be arbitration treaties whenever both parties think they are advisable—and this was precisely the opinion that most even of my own good friends in the Senate took as regards the last batch of arbitration treaties which I sent them." Choate was instructed to seek "obligatory arbitration as broad in scope as now appears to be practicable."

Root brought American proposals at the conference in line with the central feature in his own thinking. He wanted the existing system of ad hoc arbitration to be transformed along more purely judicial lines. Root and many other international lawyers had long been troubled by the quasi-political nature of ad hoc arbitration, the tendency for nationally appointed arbiters to follow the path of diplomatic necessity rather than judicial

impartiality in reaching their decisions, to split the political difference whether the law required it or not. What was needed, the lawyer-reformers believed, was a permanent and continuous court whose judges, as Root urged at the time, would be "dominated solely by jurisprudence" and be "unaffected by national and diplomatic considerations."

Roosevelt endorsed Root's objective but never had high expectations for the second Hague Conference. A tepid American conference diplomacy was the result. In the end, a conference riddled with controversy produced little practical advance for arbitration. The lack of progress, owing largely to German-led opposition, was naturally coupled with a resoundingly hollow rededication to the principle of arbitration. Choate said some years afterwards that the American proposal for a general arbitration treaty evoked "intense interest" and "was the one question which became critical, if you believe that any question could be said to be critical, but in respect to which . . . there were violent differences of opinion."

Choate recalled that thirty-two of the nations present had approved of the treaty, but that one nation—presumably Germany—had threatened to withdraw from the conference if final action on the pro-

posal was pressed. Root put a good face on the results with limp clichés. "In a good cause a good fight bravely lost is always a victory," he said at one point. In the aftermath of the conference, he told Carnegie that it was time to get "the arbitration business on its legs again." Root then negotiated his own web of twenty-five bilateral arbitration treaties in 1908 in a form he knew would be acceptable to the Senate, and the Senate ratified them. Ever the gradualist, Root was sure that doing the possible was better than doing nothing at all.

Few of Carnegie's new trustees had the practical experience that Choate, Foster, White, and certainly Root had garnered in arbitration diplomacy. But they were involved in other ways. Albert Smiley, as early as 1895, had converted his conference center into what would become, over the years, a singularly prominent annual forum, the Lake Mohonk Conferences on International Arbitration. A badge of respectability was one of the things Smiley wanted most for these gatherings. He circumscribed their work with strenuous discipline. Arbitration, and only arbitration, was a proper subject for dis-

cussion. Not war, per se, because that would be too controversial. Not peace, per se, because that might associate the Mohonk deliberations with what some conferees regarded as less respectable peace activism. A report on the first decade of Mohonk meetings proudly asserted that the conference had "secured the attention and co-operation of a once skeptical press ... it has the respect of the American public, many of whose recognized leaders are enrolled as its members ... it has to a very great degree replaced with confidence the former general distrust with which it was looked upon by the government at Washington."

Foster was twice president of the Mohonk Conference during the first decade, and Butler played a leading role during these years, particularly as president in 1909. Butler also worked hard to create institutional links with Europeans interested in arbitration, and these ties would, in the decades ahead, serve as one of the foundations for Butler's activities on behalf of the Carnegie Endowment. The Mohonk deliberations in 1903 were a sign of the times. "Why Business Men Should Promote International Arbitration" was

the subject that year. Their conviction that they should promote it led soon thereafter to the formation of the New York Peace Society.

The society became a principal national organization for business interests favoring arbitration and a foreign policy oriented toward the peaceful settlement of international problems. Its first president was Oscar Straus and its second was Carnegie. Its directors included prominent financiers like George Perkins, who later headed the finance committee of the Carnegie Endowment. The society's members included Root and Choate, and combined a cross section of the primarily Republican corporate and financial communities in New York with weighty representation from New York educational, religious, and philanthropic groups.

Straus himself was no stranger to arbitration. He had been involved in bilateral arbitral diplomacy while representing the United States in Turkey. He had campaigned for appointment as an American "judge" on the first Hague Court, and in 1902 Roosevelt gave him the appointment, despite initial reluctance because of Straus's Democratic party background.

During the Venezuela crisis that year Straus had urged Roosevelt to arbitrate the case at The Hague rather than accept, as he considered doing, the personal intermediary role that had been urged upon him. Straus's advice was geared not only to promote arbitration but also to protect Roosevelt. Political damage in the hemisphere, Straus reasoned, would have been inevitable for the president if he agreed to diplomatic mediation and then decided against Venezuela, whereas German antagonism and possible German counterpressures in the Western Hemisphere would have been risked by a decision in Venezuela's favor. Later, Straus worked behind the scenes and publicly to secure support for Roosevelt's bilateral arbitration treaties, and he was bitterly disappointed when they were gutted by the Senate.

A powerful push for arbitration also came, largely in anticipation of the second Hague peace conference, from the nation's international lawyers. Prominent members of the New York Bar Association had become convinced by the Venezuela crisis in 1895 that a more legally sound approach to arbitration was required. They and other lawyers joined together in 1906 to create the American Society of International Law, still today their leading professional association. The society's founders included James Brown Scott, one of the foremost proponents of arbitration reform, as well as Foster, Montague, Straus, and White. The first president of the society was the ubiquitous Root.

Others among the original Carnegie Endowment trustees developed connections to the arbitration movement at the turn of the century. Eliot, who along with Carnegie actively participated in the anti-imperialist campaign after the Spanish-American War, had already begun in the 1890s to speak out in favor of arbitration. "War does not often settle disputes, while arbitration always does," he once declared with characteristic certitude. He remained a strong booster throughout his later years.

Montague, when he became more involved in international matters after his gubernatorial years, was an original member and subsequently president of one of the most prestigious proarbitration groups, the American Society for the Judicial Settlement of International Disputes. The society was established during the Taft presidency, with the endorsement of both the president and Secretary Knox, just a month or so before Taft delivered his proarbitration speech at the Hotel Astor in New York in March 1910. Dominated by prominent international lawyers—Scott was its first president and Choate later a vice president—the group was organized specifically to promote the idea of a permanent and properly judicial court of arbitration. The inaugural international meeting of the society was the setting for Taft's second major policy address on the subject of arbitration and a speech by Carnegie, only days after the establishment of the Carnegie Endowment.

"When Mr. Carnegie's Money is Gone"

Carnegie as "The Steel King" and "The Sower"

CARNEGIE SAYS NO

In the opening years of the century, Carnegie began giving away his fortune, as he had promised to do. Humorists had a field day poking fun. Newspapers dutifully published updates on how much money he actually dispensed. Seekers of his benefactions sprang up, it seemed, on every street corner, in every university, and among proselytizers, for an endless roster of causes, silly and serious alike. One shrewd observer said that they all wanted his money, but did not necessarily want his philanthropy. Twain discerned this truth with utter clarity. "Dear Sir and Friend," he wrote with mock formality—the two men often corresponded as "Saint Andrew" and "Saint Mark"—"You seem to be prosperous these days. Could you lend an admirer a dollar and a half to buy a hymn-book with? God will bless you if you do; I feel it, I know it. So will I. If there should be other applications this one not to count. . . . P.S. Don't send the hymn-book, send the money. I want to make the selection myself."

The stories are legion of how difficult it was even for the worthiest of claimants—even those who most cleverly packaged and timed their importunings— to get what they wanted from the tightfisted Scotsman. We catch a glimpse of the contest between benefactor and supplicant in the conversation between two successful applicants, pleased with having received money for a major university, yet drained by the cajoling it took: "Didn't you feel," one of them asked, "you were playing a salmon? You'd get it up near by and then he'd rush off again." His companion, the university president, replied: "I'll tell you how I felt. I felt like backing him up in the corner and saying, 'Give it!' And then I kept saying to myself, 'It's his money, it's his money.'" Carnegie's leading biographer has written that by the middle of the decade "Carnegie was tired of the game, and by 1910 he was desperately sick of it." And to a close friend, Carnegie lamented: "The final dispensation of one's wealth preparing for the final exit is I found a heavy task—all sad— . . . You have no idea the strain I have been under."

As it happened, the campaign emanating from various quarters to convince Carnegie to donate generously to the cause of peace peaked during the years 1906-1910. There is no evidence that these particular claimants added disproportionally to the philanthropist's frustrations over his wealth-giving during those years, but they certainly felt the frustration of being unable to find the key that would unlock the door to a major benefaction. They never did find it. Carnegie was saying no or maybe to them right up to the time that Taft made his March 1910 speech. When he did say yes, he said it not to them, but to his own private instinct that the moment of opportunity for practical action had arrived—practicality being precisely what he had found wanting in the proposals he previously rejected. Once he made his decision he paid virtually no attention to the specific contents of these earlier proposals. He did not even mention them in his correspondence during the months of feverish preparations leading to the creation of the Endowment in December.

POUR
L'ARBITRAGE

米國アンドリュー・カーネーキー著

日本 都筑馨六 譯

國際平和論

大日本平和協會出版部

Carnegie's views on peace and arbitration were known worldwide. This is a Japanese translation of one of his major addresses.

The Carnegie Institution of Washington, at right, established in 1902. In its board room, eight years later, Carnegie assembled the trustees of hi[s] new peace endowment.

*A*merica's favorite humorist early in this century was Finley Peter Dunne, whose voice was that of the homespun and thoroughly irreverent Irish barkeep, Mr. Dooley. Carnegie and peace were two subjects he could not resist.

I like Andhrew Carnaygie. Him an' me ar-re agreed on that point. I like him because he ain't shamed to give publicly. Ye don't find him puttin' on false whiskers an' turnin' up his coat-collar whin he goes out to be benivolent. No, sir. Ivry time he dhrops a dollar it makes a noise like a waither fallin' down-stairs with a tray iv dishes. He's givin' th' way we'd all like to give. I niver put annything in th' poor-box, but I wud if Father Kelly wud rig up like wan iv thim slot-machines, so that whin I stuck in a nickel me name wud appear over th' altar in red letthers. . . . Him that giveth to th' poor, they say, lindeth to th' Lord; but in these days we look fr quick returns on our invistmints. I like Andhrew Carneygie, an', as he says, he puts his whole soul into th' wurruk.

Mr. Dooley did not see much good, however, in the second Hague Conference.

Th' convintion thin discussed a risolution offered be th' Turkish dillygate abolishin' war altogether. This also was carrid, on'y England, France, Rooshya, Germany, Italy, Austhree, Japan, an' th' United States votin' no. This made th' way fr th' discussion iv th' larger question iv how future wars shud be conducted in th' best inthrests iv peace. . . . Th' Hon'rable Joe Choate moved that in future wars horses shud be fed with hay wheriver possible. Carrid.

Th' entire South American dillygation said that no nation ought to go to war because another national wanted to put a bill on th' slate. Th' English dillygate was much incensed. 'Why, gintlemen," says he, "if ye deprived us iv th' right to collect debts be killin th' debtor ye wud take away fr'm war its entire moral purpose. I must ask ye again to cease thinkin' on this subjick in a gross mateeryal way an' considher th' moral side alone," he says. Th' conference was much moved be this pathetic speech, th' dillygate fr'm France wept softly into his hankerchef, an' th' dillygate fr'm Germany wint over an' forcibly took an openface goold watch fr'm th' dillygate fr'm Vinzwara.

MONEY FOR PEACE: THE EARLIEST PROPOSALS

Twice in 1900 and again in 1902, Carnegie's acquaintances suggested to him in a very general way that the cause of peace deserved his financial backing. Although he was willing to finance an assortment of peace-related activities, he declined throughout the first half of the decade to support a single-purpose benefaction with a peace mandate. During this period, however, he did set up American trusts dedicated to the fields of science, with the establishment of the Carnegie Institution of Washington in 1902, and education, with the creation of the Carnegie Foundation for the Advancement of Teaching in 1905. He also enriched his beloved Pittsburgh, home to the young Carnegie and to his fortune, with the creation of the Carnegie Institute and the Carnegie Institute of Technology.

By the time other Carnegie acquaintances tried again after the middle of the decade, the American outlook on the world had broadened. Public interest in foreign affairs had grown, and organizations representing internationalist and peace constituencies had proliferated during the Roosevelt years. Roosevelt himself was the catalyst for many of these changes. Like his presidency overall, his diplomacy

was larger than life. He played hero, bully, statesman, peacemaker, and even philosopher. He was lionized and criticized for his foreign policy. But Americans could not ignore it. They could not but pay more and more attention to what was going on in the world, shedding in the process their nineteenth-century cocoon of isolation and indifference. And with the entry of the organized peace movement into the political mainstream, those who earlier had been unable to persuade Carnegie to finance a peace organization judged that their prospects might be brighter during the second half of the decade.

The author of the 1902 approach to Carnegie was Edwin Mead, a scholarly, prominent peace crusader from Boston. He petitioned Carnegie again in 1905, urging him to endow generously a clearinghouse for publishing and disseminating peace literature. The idea had little appeal to

Carnegie, and he tried to make clear that a permanent peace endowment needed a more definite and attractive rationale. "If we could only get the effective organization," he wrote to Mead, "the funds would be forthcoming. So far the path does not seem clear to me but it may be revealed."

Another peace leader of the day tried a different tack, thinking that Carnegie's recent experience in creating the Carnegie Institution in Washington might serve as a model. The proposal was to create separate Carnegie organizations in England, France, and Germany, all aimed at promoting a peace-seeking alliance among these three countries and the United States. Carnegie, in his much-publicized rectorial address to the students of the University of St. Andrews in 1905, had proposed a five-power League of Peace—adding Russia as the fifth member. So this latest proposal might have been expected

to strike a responsive chord. But for Carnegie the results-oriented philanthropist, the plan held no interest as a practical venture.

Another suggestion came in early 1907 from a second Bostonian, the wealthy textbook publisher Edwin Ginn, later founder of the World Peace Foundation. After an initial interview with Carnegie, Ginn decided to flatter him, writing that the meeting was the first time in his life that he had "ever met a man who knew in a broad way what ought to be done in this great peace cause and at the same time was financially able to carry out these plans." Ginn proposed that they join together to raise $10 million for a permanent peace organization and offered somewhat tentatively to put up as much as $1 million "as soon as I can get hold of my funds." Like his close adviser Mead, Ginn was mainly interested in promoting education and information projects aimed at a wide public. The flattery did not help; neither did the narrow educational focus. The path Carnegie needed had yet to be "revealed."

Enter Nicholas Murray Butler. Well-known in peace-activist circles as being a friend of Carnegie's and an important collaborator with the steelmaster in philanthropic affairs, Butler became the focal point for seekers of Carnegie's largesse who had become convinced that individual appeals from scattered sources would continue to be futile. Butler was familiar with Carnegie's way of doing things. He knew, from considerable experience, the other key players in the Carnegie circle. And he knew the way they all deferred to Root.

Butler was fond of the story of his own role in the establishment of the Carnegie Institution of Washington. Carnegie had originally wanted to set up a national university in Washington—a notion that White had suggested to him in 1900. When he later settled on the idea of an institution dedicated to scientific work, he wanted it to be a quasi-governmental body, on the model of the Smithsonian Institution. He also wanted the new president, Theodore Roosevelt, to be an ex officio member of the board of trustees. Roosevelt jumped at the idea and was per-

suaded by Carnegie to ask Congress to pass a joint resolution establishing the institution.

Roosevelt wanted Butler's advice and called him to the President's House. (The mansion was renamed the "White House" later in Roosevelt's tenure, giving it a

more common touch to conform to the style of his presidency.) He asked Butler to write the congressional message that would be needed for the new enterprise. But Butler told him that seeking quasi-official status would be a terrible mistake. Carnegie's reputation, stained by the violent suppression of the Homestead strike by the Carnegie Steel Company at the beginning of the 1890s, Butler argued, would be dragged once more into the public eye by a muckraking press and hostile politicians in Congress. Butler was certain that the results would be disastrous for the president, for Carnegie, and for the proposed institution.

But Roosevelt would not budge. A desperate Butler pleaded with him to delay action until he consulted Root. When Roosevelt said that Root knew nothing about the subject, Butler countered that it didn't matter, his judgment should be sought anyway. The secretary of war was summoned immediately for a late-night meeting; he was told by the president that there was a difference of view, but not who held which opinion. Root read the proposed draft message, and, thinking that it came from Butler, exclaimed, "Where did this damn fool idea come from?" Butler's instinct was vindicated, and Roosevelt relented.

Carnegie's private study in New York. Stenciled on the wall are his favorite mottoes.

Bostonian Hamilton Holt, Butler's ally before 1910 in unsuccessful efforts to influence Carnegie

Finally, for those who were interested in getting Carnegie to endow a peace organization, Butler possessed another advantage. He had actually succeeded in getting money from Carnegie in 1906 for the establishment of an American branch of the Association for International Conciliation. The branch was headed by Butler. The parent organization in Paris was run by a close associate of Butler's, Baron Paul d'Estournelles de Constant, a member of the French Senate and later a Nobel Peace Prize recipient and representative of the Carnegie Endowment in Europe. His magazine, *International Conciliation,* was subsequently absorbed by the Endowment and published by it for many decades.

BUTLER'S PLAN

The most concrete effort to turn Carnegie's philanthropic energies toward peace was stimulated by Hamilton Holt, the managing editor of a leading journal, *The Independent.* Holt was an active internationalist and a proponent of ambitious schemes for international organizations. Holt and Butler were working together in 1908 on a New York Peace Society dinner

in honor of Root, when in the course of a conversation Holt referred to the example of the Carnegie Institution and the more recently created Carnegie Institute in Pittsburgh, and suggested that Butler make a specific proposal to Carnegie for a $10 million endowment devoted to the promotion of peace. Butler was interested. Correspondence and further discussion followed, during which Butler offered his own ideas about what a new organization might do. The stratagem devised by Butler was this: Holt and a few other peace organizers whom Carnegie knew, including Albert Smiley, would send a joint proposal to Butler, with supplemental endorsements of prominent figures who likewise were known to have Carnegie's confidence. Butler would then present the proposal to Carnegie.

The proposal, in the form of a letter addressed to Butler, was received by him in December 1908. The signatories noted Butler's work as president of the American branch of the Association for International Conciliation, pointed to the model of the other two major Carnegie benefactions, and proposed a similar fund. "By persistent public demonstrations," they wrote, "by the promotion of international visits and other courtesies, by the spread of literature, by the enlightenment of the people through the press, the pulpit, and the platform, and by the aiding of existing agencies, this fund would be made potent in developing a public opinion not only in America, but in Europe and Asia, that would in time reduce the martial and jingo elements of the several populations to comparative impotence. We believe that

F. ED SPOONER

"ROTOGRAPH SERIES"

ANDREW CARNEGIE IN "AUTO"

B 771

Carnegie in his touring car

Mr. Carnegie would look with favor upon such a work . . . we take the liberty of requesting you, if it seems to you proper, to confer with him, making such presentation of the matter as may seem to you wise and fitting." Signed by Holt, Mead, Smiley, and two others, the letter was accompanied by brief statements of support from Foster, White, and Root.

Butler had also had his share of disappointments with Carnegie. He had recently responded to the philanthropist's general request for advice on how to give away $5 to $10 million by suggesting that he give it to Columbia University, of which Butler was then president. Carnegie had deflected the idea. Now, writing again to Carnegie at the beginning of 1909 and enclosing the joint proposal, Butler referred discreetly to his earlier try: "I infer that that suggestion has not appealed to you favorably. Under the circumstances, therefore, I should hesitate to write you again in regard to any undertaking were it not for the fact that the ideas and suggestions contained in this enclosure seem to me so admirable and capable of such benificent

development, that I deem it my duty to place the document in your hand, with the statement that I am at your service at any time should you wish to give detailed consideration to the suggestions which these gentlemen make."

Carnegie responded three days later. "It is a matter that needs very careful and prolonged consultation. Someday when you have time we'll be glad to talk it over. At present I feel that it is too much in the air—much talk about bringing people together, and all of this sort of thing, and nothing of a definite character. The avenues of expenditure should be distinctly stated." (A year earlier another supplicant had been told, "If any peace or arbitration organization is assisted by me, it will have to show vigorous work.")

Butler had miscalculated. He and Holt began to see how tough their campaign would be. "I think on the whole his response is not unfavorable," Holt wrote to the Columbia University president, "but we apparently have gone somewhat on the wrong track." What would be necessary, he concluded, would be "to present

a practical plan to Mr. Carnegie that will be simply invincible. We shall need your help more than anyone else."

The New York Peace Society dinner for Root proceeded as planned, with Choate presiding, and with Taft, Butler, and other regulars (including Mark Twain) in the audience. By the beginning of April 1909 Butler and his collaborators were ready to try again. This time they presented Carnegie with a scheme more detailed, as well as more ambitious, than the last, under the title "Proposed Plan for the Establishment of a Carnegie International Institute." In his covering letter to Carnegie, Butler reminded him of his wish for a clearer statement and more definite plan of how the money would be spent, and said that the new proposal was formulated "with a view to complying with your suggestion."

The proposed institute would work generally toward the prevention of war, the perfection of arbitral justice, and the development of an international police force. This, one presumes, was pure Holt. The rest was pure Butler. The institute would educate world public opinion; furnish newspapers of the world with peace-promoting materials; correct misstatements of fact in the world press; link up like-minded networks of organiza-

Carnegie's extensive library in New York reflected this self-educated man's love of books.

tions worldwide; organize agents in every city of considerable size throughout the world; produce scholarly studies; and promote international exchanges of "representative individuals and groups of citizens." Carnegie could choose the degree of permanence; a five- or ten-year trial period would suffice, if the benefactor thought it prudent. "Such an institute," the proposal promised, "would speedily become not only the center of the whole peace movement of the world, but also a clearing-house for all organizations and currents of opinions" involved in the pursuit of justice. Carnegie, it seems, was not interested in anything so open-ended. This scheme may well have struck him as impossible rather than invincible.

The next strategy that was concocted was intended to appeal to Carnegie's well-known dissatisfaction with the overlap among the many peace organizations of the day, as well as to his equally well-known interest in arbitration. Once again, Butler was center stage. At Butler's urging, Root became personally involved, though marginally, for the first time. The May 1909 session of the Lake Mohonk Conference, over which Butler presided, adopted a resolution establishing a Committee of Ten, to be led by Butler. Its stated purpose was to examine the possibility of set-

ting up a national council for arbitration and peace. The committee's hidden agenda, however, was to get Carnegie to endow a permanent peace organization.

Butler wrote to Root in September, telling him that members of the committee would not be selected until he and Root had talked over the whole idea. He asked Root to help select appropriate candidates. With Root's concurrence, Butler decided in November that the committee should consist of himself, Carnegie, Root, Scott, Smiley, and others known to be in Carnegie's favor. At year's end, Butler invited Carnegie to join the group and Carnegie accepted. Only three months remained before Taft would deliver his landmark speech at the Hotel Astor.

"You are the most important member of the Committee," Butler told Root in January 1910, hoping to get him involved as deeply as possible in the new stratagem, or at least to make sure that Root associated himself with any specific proposals from the committee. But the odds were not good. Both Root and Carnegie were preoccupied with more pressing matters during the opening months of 1910. They were preoccupied with Roosevelt.

THE ROOSEVELT FACTOR

Within a month after Taft's inauguration, Roosevelt embarked on what would become a spectacular and controversial pilgrimage abroad, first on a much-publicized African safari, financed in part by Carnegie, and then on a political tour through North Africa and Europe. He returned to the United States only in June 1910.

During Roosevelt's time abroad, Taft undid important accomplishments of Roosevelt's progressive Republican legacy, and the Taft White House gradually came to be seen as a breeding place for anti-Roosevelt, anti-Progressive tendencies. Always a conservative Republican stalwart, Taft was never comfortable with the rise of progressivism within his party, and his discomfort intensified with every new battle he fought at the beginning of his presidency with the Republican insurgents, as the Progressives were known.

Root positioned himself during this period as a healer of the breach between Taft and Roosevelt, as an interpreter of one to the other, and as a guardian of his party's future against the calamity that he knew would come from their political fratricide. Root managed, during 1910, to preserve his good-faith relations with both Taft and Roosevelt, not yet having to

During early 1910, Carnegie was planning a private diplomatic initiative for Theodore Roosevelt, then on a safari in Africa. A cartoonist imagined Roosevelt's arrival producing this reaction in the African bush...

face the painful question of what he would do if and when their breach widened beyond repair.

During the first half of 1910, both Carnegie and Root corresponded with Roosevelt in Africa about a remarkable excursion of the steelmaster's into the world of high-stakes private diplomacy. It centered on the German kaiser, Wilhelm II, and it dominated Carnegie's attention that spring. The idea had probably originated from a seed that Roosevelt himself had planted in Carnegie's mind back in the summer of 1906. Roosevelt was then planning for the forthcoming Hague peace conference. Flushed with the recent success of his spectacular personal mediation of a peace settlement between Russia and Japan in 1905—the Nobel Peace Prize went to Roosevelt the next year—he wrote Carnegie: "Do you know, I sometimes wish that we did not have the ironclad custom which forbids a President ever to go abroad? If I could meet the Kaiser and the responsible authorities of France and England, I think I could be of help in this Hague Conference business."

Roosevelt's willingness even to entertain the idea of personal diplomacy with the kaiser at that time reflected a less anti-German attitude on his part than was prevalent in Washington's political and diplomatic establishment. Nineteenth-century Americans had admired German scientific and industrial accomplishments, constitutionalism and culture, and educational and philosophical contributions to Western thought. But as America's entente with the British grew, its pro-German sentiments at official levels waned, all the more so as German imperial and economic designs increasingly confronted American interests around the world.

Some prominent Americans, Butler, Charlemagne Tower, and White among them, remained confident at the turn of the century that Germany could overcome its militarist and aggressive tendencies. They also remained hopeful that the erratic autocrat sitting so pompously on the German throne could be counted on as a man of peace. Roosevelt knew that German power and ambition were a potential threat to European stability, and he also knew from his own indirect diplomatic encounters with the kaiser that Germany could be swayed by American diplomacy. That the kaiser's ambassador to Washington, Speck von Sternburg, was one of Roosevelt's intimates contributed in no small degree to Roosevelt's measured view of Washington's relations with Berlin and to his wish to maintain a calculated friendship with the kaiser.

Carnegie's plan for Roosevelt in 1910 has been dubbed "a little Hague Conference of his own." Roosevelt would meet with the kaiser to discuss measures for ameliorating mounting tensions in Europe, reach some broad understandings if possible, and then go to England, where he would confer with British officials under the cover of a contrived social event at Wrest Park, the country residence of the American ambassador. President Taft blessed the venture in advance, and Carnegie, Roosevelt, and Root, together worked out a script for the former President to follow. Had Carnegie been able to have his own way in the matter, he and Root would have gone to Berlin to join Roosevelt and the kaiser, but Root said he was unable to go and Carnegie dropped the idea. "There is really your Big Game," Carnegie wrote Roosevelt in Africa, referring to the encounter in Berlin that was

...and with good reason.

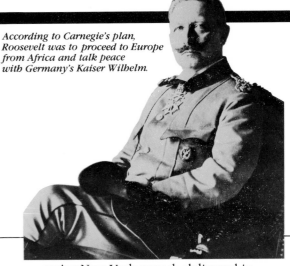

According to Carnegie's plan, Roosevelt was to proceed to Europe from Africa and talk peace with Germany's Kaiser Wilhelm.

planned for May. Root was decidedly more cautious, and Carnegie knew why.

Earlier, in 1909, socialists in the Reichstag had asked the German foreign secretary why the kaiser had failed to conclude an arbitration treaty with the United States. His answer implied that the fault was Washington's. Root, out of office then, wrote Carnegie a confidential letter bristling with anger at the Germans. "The fact is that I proposed to Germany to make the same treaty which we made with England, France, Italy, Austria and practically all the rest of the world except Russia, and Germany refused to make it. . . . Speck von Sternburg wanted to make the treaty and he did his best to make his government agree to it, but the German Foreign Office, which is a narrow, bureaucratic survival of the Eighteenth Century, never had the slightest idea of making a treaty. I told

Speck that the German people would not like it when they found they were left alone with Russia while all the rest of the world had climbed on to the arbitration wagon with us, and he realized it. . . . The fact is, and no well informed person can doubt it, that Germany, under her present government, is the great disturber of peace in the world. . . . She looks with real contempt and loathing upon the whole system of arbitration, and she considers all talk about it to be mere hypocrisy." Nonetheless, Carnegie's new project at least held out for Root the possibility of circumventing what he regarded as the obstructive German Foreign Office.

Carnegie had had his own exposure to the kaiser earlier in the decade. He had spoken often, and usually with unvarnished optimism, about his hopes for the kaiser as peacemaker, most pointedly in a

major New York speech delivered in 1907. Carnegie also possessed good personal connections of his own in Germany. He was virtually destined to end up sooner or later as one of the many Anglo-American visitors that trooped, on invitation, to the kaiser's yacht at the Kiel Regatta every summer. The 1907 speech had stimulated an invitation from the emperor, and Carnegie had accepted eagerly.

Carnegie's private meetings with the kaiser had led nowhere, but their jocular moments hinted at what would become Carnegie's hopes in the 1910 episode. Carnegie was not alone in seeing personal similarities between Roosevelt and the kaiser, and he told the kaiser so. The resemblance had also suggested itself to Butler during his first meeting with the kaiser two years earlier, a meeting Butler described as very much like a chat among friends in the privacy of the Century club in New York. Carnegie told the kaiser that he would like to hitch the two leaders together in the cause of peace. "Ah, I see!" the kaiser replied. "You want to drive us. Roosevelt will be in front and I behind." "No, Your Majesty," Carnegie said. "I know better than to drive such wild colts tandem. You never get enough purchase on the first horse. No, I would like to have you both in the shafts, holding you abreast."

"Medal to the Only Peaceful Monarch." This 1907 cartoon was prompted by a celebrated Carnegie speech praising the German emperor.

"Getting Nervous as Teddy Approaches." So nervous was the German Foreign Office that it derailed Roosevelt's plans.

"Neither Root, Butler, nor I," Carnegie wrote Roosevelt during the planning for the Berlin meeting, "are 'peace at any price' men; while we might be the last to draw the sword, if compelled to do so we should be among the last to sheathe it." Roosevelt expressed reservations—but gently—to the man who, after all, was helping to pay for his safari. "With *your* policy, as you outline it (of course accepting it generally and not binding myself as to details), I am in hearty sympathy; what Root champions along those lines you can guarantee I will champion also."

Roosevelt then added a crucial passage about peace and arbitration. "My past words," Roosevelt explained, "and the acts wherein I have striven to make those words good, afford proof of my sincerity in the cause of peace. I will do all I can to bring about such a league of, or understanding among, the great powers as will forbid one of them, or any small power, to engage in unrighteous, foolish or needless war; to secure an effective arbitral tribunal, with power to enforce at least certain of its decrees; to secure an agreement to check the waste of money on growing and excessive armaments. If, as is probable, so much cannot be secured at

once, I will do all I can to help in the movement, rapid or slow, towards the desired end. But I will not be, and you would not wish me to be, put in the attitude of advocating the impossible, or, above all, of seeming to be insincere. For instance, as Root will tell you, no arbitration or other agreement would ever make the American people even for a moment consider the question of submitting to arbitration its right to exclude Asiatics.... Root ... and I know that under no circumstances would there be (and there ought not to be) the remotest chance of securing the ratification by the Senate of any general treaty or agreement which would leave such a matter as this to be decided by anybody but ourselves ... I cannot be, or seem to be, an accredited envoy; I cannot work for a policy which I think our country might repudiate; I cannot work for anything that does not represent some real

progress.... In France, Italy, Austria and Germany—especially Germany—I shall go into the matter at length with the men of power, and I will report to you in full in England."

Root's clinical realism weighed in next, in a letter written to Carnegie for transmission to Roosevelt: "The crux of the whole matter is in Berlin, and there is one thing and only one thing that can be done there so far as I can see. That is to say to the Emperor: 'One of those great opportunities which have been presented to a very few men in history lies before you at this moment.... The opportunity is to do this: That you, having the greatest and most effective army that ever existed in the world, having the means and the constructive capacity and great advances already made for an unsurpassed navy, shall say to the world, "I will lead you to peace. Let us stop where we are, and let us end now and

The "Two Doves of Peace" did meet, but did not play the roles Carnegie had envisaged for them.

here the race of competition in enlargement of provision for war" ' . . . . The only way to quit is to quit. The Emperor can do it, and no one else can. If he does it he will win everlasting renown. If he does not avail himself of the opportunity he will go down in history just like the ordinary kings and generals that you can pick up by the wagon load from the pages of any universal history. I don't know of anybody who would be more likely to make a lodgement in the Emperor's mind with this idea than Theodore Roosevelt."

Writing to Carnegie from the White Nile, Roosevelt was upbeat: "I shall use both your letter and Root's with the Kaiser; they are exactly what I wished. I also have a letter from Root to me which I shall show you. How wise he is! and what a good friend to both you and me! If you see him tell him I shall be exceedingly careful not to fall into the errors against which he warns me. . . . What an interesting meeting we shall have at Wrest Park!" Carnegie tried to circumvent Root's caution, telling Roosevelt: "I think that friend Root does not quite grasp your position, which is unique. No man in history has ever occupied it before and you should speak out your mind fully. . . . The bolder you are, the better."

Root's reaction to what happened next

is not recorded, but he must have had a sense of déjà vu, remembering his previous experience with the German Foreign Office. Having learned of Roosevelt's agenda with the kaiser, the Foreign Office saw to it that the Berlin press unloaded an avalanche of anti-Americanism in anticipation of Roosevelt's arrival. (Roosevelt later told a friend that he suspected that the plan had been leaked "through some inadvertence on Mr. Carnegie's part.") "If, as I suppose to be the case, you have seen the Berlin papers," Roosevelt wrote to Carnegie from Paris at the end of April 1910, "you probably already know that even my anticipations of the difficulties came far short of the actual facts." Then, just before Roosevelt's arrival in Germany, official state matters in Europe were interrupted by the death of England's King Edward VII and a subsequent period of mourning. Roosevelt did manage to meet

with the kaiser, but had been forewarned after the Foreign Office's alert to the press that there must be no discussion of arms limitation or arbitration. The meeting at Wrest Park never took place.

While Carnegie and Root had been plotting with Roosevelt, Butler's efforts to move forward with the work of the Committee of Ten had sputtered because of various logistical difficulties that prevented meetings from being arranged. In April 1910 Butler offered his own conclusions independently to Carnegie: "I would establish at Washington a Bureau under a competent and active head, for the purpose of keeping members of Congress accurately informed regarding the movement for peace and arbitration." Work "on . . . [the] international side," Butler urged, should be left to the Association for International Conciliation, that is, to d'Estournelles and himself. Butler was

willing to let educational work be conducted by Ginn in Boston, and peace "propaganda and agitation" by a reorganized New York Peace Society.

Butler assured Carnegie that the whole concept was "simple, economical, and would avoid duplication"—problems about which he knew Carnegie was concerned. In view of the relationship between the two men, it is not surprising that Butler would have assumed so central a role for himself. It may have surprised Butler, however, that this letter, like others that preceded it, attracted no apparent enthusiasm from Carnegie.

Roosevelt had received many letters from Carnegie while in Europe, among them one sent in April. Carnegie had written that the Republican party was undergoing "the usual dissentions in a party which has just conquered, but they are not deep. On the whole, the administration is making good.... It is astonishing what a hold you have" in the Western states, Carnegie said. "The mere mention of your name brought an outburst from every person in the audience. I never saw anything like it. I hope and pray when you return that you will be able to preserve an impartial attitude and take no part whatever in the differences of party, just standing aloof. President Taft justifies the confi-

dence and support of every loyal Republican, and will continue to do so."

Then he mentioned Taft's March arbitration speech. "I rejoice that the President has put our country in the van—the first land to proclaim that all disputes must be settled. If you back him up, we shall win, go on conquering." Carnegie had forgotten, or chose to pretend that he had forgotten, the long and frank letter he had received only two months earlier in which Roosevelt bared his thoughts about arbitration. Carnegie would not again see those thoughts in print over Roosevelt's signature for another year. When he did, the entire nation would see them as well, and Carnegie's infant peace endowment would be caught up in the political maelstrom resulting from the former president's final and most important foray into the controversy over arbitration.

CARNEGIE DECIDES

Myths about Carnegie abound, as they do often with men who are so difficult to explain by conventional standards. One of the most durable was the belief that his most important business decisions were the result of sheer, sudden inspiration, an almost mystical moment of revelation that pointed him to what must be done. This is how, according to some accounts, he was supposed to have made the critical decision to make use of the Bessemer conversion process to turn iron into steel, the foundation of his industrial empire. It did not happen this way at all, as Carnegie's biographer has shown. It happened because Carnegie experimented, considered alternatives, waited for the pieces to fall into place, and then trusted his instinct when the moment seemed right.

Roosevelt came home to a hero's welcome in June 1910. While in Africa, he had written Carnegie about his hostility to unconditional arbitration—precisely what Taft had proposed as his peace policy several months earlier.

One secondhand account has Carnegie deciding to create the Endowment while playing golf at Skibo in the summer of 1910.

Carnegie was not averse to sustaining this myth, however. He said that he realized the truth of Herbert Spencer's philosophy in just such a flash of revelatory insight. In the summer of 1910, according to one later, secondhand account, "the exact form" that the benefaction he intended to make for peace "came to him suddenly, like a revelation, on the golf links at Skibo." Like much of Carnegie lore, this is impossible to verify. Yet all indications are, in fact, that Carnegie did not decide until that summer to set up a new institution, and that his decision was essentially a solo one.

During a hectic year lasting from October 1910 to October 1911, the story unfolded of how the Carnegie Endowment came to be, what the founder wanted, and what happened with his personal agenda.

October 28, 1910

Taft writes Carnegie inviting him and Mrs. Carnegie to visit the White House for an overnight stay. "That will give you and me," the President says, "an opportunity to discuss the matter you mention in your note."

The secretary of the Committee of Ten wrote Carnegie in the third week in October, forwarding another draft plan for the contemplated national council and inviting him to make suggestions in advance of another meeting. The letter reveals no awareness that Carnegie was pursuing on his own another course of action entirely. For Carnegie, the continuing efforts of the Committee of Ten had become a sideshow. He was now about to plunge into the month and a half of maneuvering to seal his bargain with Taft.

Root was becoming steadily more engaged on Carnegie's behalf with both the president and Knox. He also was at this time heavily involved in domestic political matters, and Roosevelt was much on his mind. The former president had returned in June to a hero's welcome and to a political arena rife with signs of deepening trouble for the Taft administration. "Teddy, come home and blow your horn," a popular national magazine teased. "The sheep's in the meadow, the cow's in the corn. The boy you left to 'tend the sheep is under the haystack fast asleep."

At the end of the summer Roosevelt gave what has been described as the most radical speech of his life, the famous "New Nationalism" address delivered during a rousing political swing through the American West. Devoted exclusively to domestic economic and social issues, the speech was progressivism stretched far. Another Roosevelt speech during the tour attacked judicial concepts holy to conservatives, and especially to Taft. Root saw what was happening and sought to soften the ideological and personal tensions between Taft and Roosevelt. In September Root had written this diagnosis: "The difference between them is the natural difference between a man of a reflective cast of mind with the training of a lawyer and a judge, and a man of intense activity who has led a life of physical and literary adventure."

Root heard guardedly reassuring words from Roosevelt, particularly in a long let-

Roosevelt and Taft began pulling the Republican party in different directions. Their differences became sharper as Roosevelt spoke out on domestic issues.

ter in October on the stationery of *The Outlook,* which was the former President's major outlet for public affairs writing. "I do not see," he told his friend, "how I could as a decent citizen have avoided taking the stand I have taken this year. . . . I should infinitely have preferred to keep wholly out of politics. . . . I have on every occasion this year praised everything I conscientiously could of both Taft and the Congress, and I have never said a word in condemnation of either, strongly though I have felt. Very possibly circumstances will be such that I shall support Taft for the Presidency next time. . . . I assume that you are his cordial supporter."

For Taft, the summer had brought ominous political news as administration-backed Republicans suffered an almost unbroken string of primary defeats at the hands of progressive challengers. In November, one of the dramatic mid-term political tidal waves in American electoral history confirmed these trends. It brought a Democratic majority to the House of Representatives and left a weakened Republican majority in the Senate, held hostage by newly victorious insurgent members in the party ranks. The Republican debacle sent Roosevelt into temporary eclipse, sent Taft into a desperate search for ways to redeem his leadership

before 1912, and sent a university president and Democrat named Woodrow Wilson to the governor's mansion in New Jersey.

November 3, 1910

Carnegie scribbles the draft of a deed of trust for his new benefaction. "I believ that the shortest and easiest path to peace lies in adopting President Taft's policy," he wrote, before quoting the president's March speech. "The Trustees will please begin by pressing forward this line, testing it thoroly and douting not."

A day later he wrote to Morley about his "new idea." Root and Carnegie had begun the month by corresponding about possible trustees for the new organization. Carnegie soon took the president fully into his confidence, writing him on November 8 and telling him that he had seen Root and Butler, as well as two other advisers, and that "all of them are intensely interested in the matter." He informed the president that in the draft of his deed of trust he had proposed a role for a congressional commission which had been set up that year. The commission was to "suggest" to the president that he bring the subject of arbitration agreements before Congress,

and express the desire of the Republic to negotiate for this purpose. "I beg you to consider whether in your forthcoming message you should not refer to this important action," Carnegie wrote. "I shall try to see Secretary Knox before you return."

Carnegie, on November 11, sent Knox a working draft of the deed of trust and asked him to become a member of the board of trustees. "Personally, I should like much to have you," he told the secretary. "I believ you have it in your power before you leave office, to bring about an arbitration treaty with Great Britain." He assured Knox that the British government would welcome such a move, and with his eye on Republican fortunes added: "From a party point of view, I know of no issue so important. . . . We could deluge the Senate with petitions to approve the president's recommendation, if he made it. . . . You would take care to show that it was not with Britain alone we wisht a treaty."

Three days later Carnegie sent his first round of letters inviting potential trustees to join the board, but he did not send them the draft deed of trust. And then, in a letter, or rather a draft letter, that remains one of the most peculiar Carnegie communications of that month, he shared his plans with Roosevelt. "Have decided upon

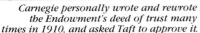

Carnegie personally wrote and rewrote the Endowment's deed of trust many times in 1910, and asked Taft to approve it.

Between October and December, Carnegie sealed his bargain with Taft. Closely involved were Root and Knox. The four men stand together in this 1910 photograph.

my $10,000,000 fund for international peace cause. President Taft, Honorary President. Elihu Root—your Elihu—President, Choate, Eliot and many of your friends trustees," Carnegie wrote. Then he added: "I thought of asking you to be a trustee but this seemed too small for you and besides I feared you might dislike to refuse, so I kept you free. If you ever wished to join very easy to arrange." On second thought, or perhaps on the basis of advice, Carnegie deleted the last sentence from the draft. The prudence of the deletion was nothing short of divine.

During these weeks Carnegie made many revisions to the working draft of the deed of trust, all of them revealing. At first, he had considered indicating in the trust that the money could, under some circumstances, be used for political purposes. "No part of this fund," he wrote in a section later deleted, "is to be used for sectarian or party purposes, but should one party ever stand for mesures leading to international peace"—and he doubtless had arbitration in mind here—"and the other against this, contributions may

be made to the former.... Any contributions so made, however, are to be widely publisht and the reason therefor given."

At another point Carnegie considered deed language that would specify alternative approaches to the negotiation of an arbitration treaty. His draft language stated that if Taft failed for some reason to press Congress to accept unconditional arbitration, as he had endorsed it in March, then the president should consider a conditional approach. "It seems so clear to me," he added in another passage that did not survive the final revision, "that rapid and decided progress toward the reign of peace can best be made by proper effort in this direction that I beg my Trustees to start upon this line."

As the end of November approached, Carnegie was pleased with the momentum, writing Scott that "even Senator Root is showing evidence of unusual impetuosity in his desire to be at the work." Keeping abreast of Carnegie's doings was not always easy for Root, as shown in one episode concerning the secretary of state.

Knox was the architect of heavy-handed and paternalistic policies in Latin America that Root saw as the undoing of his own hemispheric diplomacy. The secretary wrote Carnegie with an idea he had persuaded the president to endorse. Carnegie's board of trustees should be broadened to include a Canadian and representatives from Central and South America. Carnegie liked the idea. "It is splendid," he responded immediately, "and I shall act upon it. Senator Root is to be here this afternoon and I know he will highly approve. Now, could you suggest to me the important names to have...." Carnegie also told Knox that Root was coming to Washington to discuss the new endowment, and said he was waiting for "the President and you [to] approve the drafts I sent."

Root got Carnegie to reconsider. The next day Carnegie wrote again to Knox, telling him that Root "changed my views in regard to having anything but our own people" on the board; Root would explain when he was in Washington.

December 11, 1910

Carnegie's plans are set. Taft writes: "I . . . have read over the letter of trust, which I entirely approve. I shall be very glad to accept the position of Honorary President."

Root's meetings in Washington with the president and Knox produced another change of mind, this time on Knox's part. He wrote Carnegie on December 4: "After talking with Mr. Root I am of the opinion that it would be better if the Secretary of State were not a member of your organization." "The President," Root wrote Carnegie on December 7, "evidently wanted him in, and said so. I said to both of them that, in my judgment, the circumstances did not demand his staying out of the trusteeship but would justify it if he thought it wise. He tells me that he has written you saying he has concluded not to become a trustee. I think I should have come to the same conclusion."

Here were all of the Root trademarks. Elegantly judicious, leaving no doubt as to his own preference, he left room for others to adopt his conclusions as their own. He explained to Carnegie that "the action of the trustees might embarrass the State Department if the Secretary were a member of the Board. This is what Knox had in mind." Furthermore, "it might hamper the usefulness of the trustees if they were regarded abroad as being a mere annex of the American State Department. . . ." Root then gave Carnegie several minor technical changes in the draft deed of trust—apparently Root's sole contribution to the deed. All of the organizational preparations needed before announcing the new organization to the world seven days later were now completed.

Carnegie used the intervening days to prime the president, encouraging him to do his utmost to fulfill his part of the bargain. "You will note," Carnegie wrote Taft on December 10, "that your noble note of leadership . . . prompted me to create the fund. It is based upon your words." Carnegie offered advice on how the president might turn his general policy declaration on arbitration into a specific policy. "Perhaps your best plan," Carnegie said, "is to take up the Olney Pauncefote Treaty making needed changes if any and present it to the present Senate for ratification."

Carnegie knew better than to tell the president that he was in political trouble. Rather: "You have gained steadily thruout your whole Presidential career as a pure, zealous, steady going character from every point of view, a universal favorite with the intelligent, but there is needed for *effective* reputation among the masses some grandly bold forward step. Nothing Commonplace will do. Now the outstanding announcement so far in your career without question is your doctrine of International Arbitration of all questions."

And he knew better than to forget domestic politics. "Consider what the position of the Democratic party would be," Carnegie continued, "if the Senate failed to ratify the treaty." Carnegie then put a finer point on it. "You have it at hand certain—Excuse me for presuming to tender counsel, you can justly charge it to an intense desire to see you occupy the Commanding position you have deserved and which entitles you not only to another term—that goes without saying—but to foremost place in history which will be yours if you stand firm in advocacy of the views you have been the first Ruler to declare."

Carnegie's effusive praise of Taft probably seemed like good tactics. It also flowed from a deeper and more genuine reverence that Carnegie displayed toward the office of the presidency, no matter who the occupant. Early in the decade he had said to Butler that he had known a number of men before they became president and that once they took office he

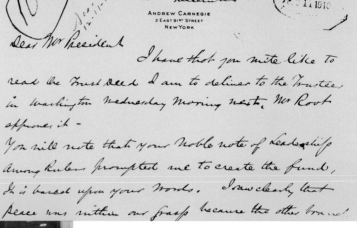

Four days before publicly announcing the creation of the Endowment on December 14, 1910, Carnegie informed Taft that all was ready and that the fund was "based upon your words."

found himself in awe of each of them.

When Carnegie finished reading his deed of trust to his assembled trustees on the morning of December 14, he spoke only about Taft and his arbitration policy. There is no evidence that any but a handful of these trustees knew the extent of Carnegie's dealings with the president during the preceding weeks. Referring to arbitration, the founder observed, "I know beyond all question, and would stake my fortune, stake my life, stake my hope of eternal salvation on the statement, that Britain stands anxious, and that all that is needed is a word from President Taft, whom I have followed. He has only to say

the word, and the responsibility upon him is great."

Carnegie emphasized the wide discretion given to his trustees by the deed—a feature of all of his major trusts—and added, "I have advised you, please notice, that you are not required to do anything, that I only hope that you will proceed in that line. There may be reasons that it is not proper just now, that it would be better to wait.... I do not believe that the Senate today would hesitate to ratify" an arbitration treaty between the United States and Great Britain, he said, and pointing to Root, he continued: "I am opposite the man who knows all about this, and I do

not.... He is inside and knows it all." Carnegie told his trustees that he was seeing the president the next afternoon.

Carnegie had brought his institution to life in less than two months. The meaning of his action, however, was almost certainly perceived in different ways by different trustees.

For those who had not had significant experience in foreign affairs, the institution most likely would have seemed to be a product mainly of the lofty sentiment that Carnegie expressed in his deed of trust, though only in a few lines. Carnegie wrote that the institution should "hasten the abolition of international war, the foulest blot upon our civilization." Spencerian that he was, he said that for man "there may be no limit short of perfection even here in this life upon erth." He stated that war could be abolished and that peace was in reach, and that after it was secured his trustees should "consider what is the next most degrading remaining evil or evils whose banishment" would advance the human cause and turn their energies toward eradicating it. He believed, and he was not far wrong, that his own aspirations meshed with the era's popular optimism, with the cheery confidence of Americans who in the years just before 1914 were devouring a best-selling series

Taft's next step came on December 17. Speaking at the New Willard Hotel in Washington (its Pennsylvania Avenue facade and elegant lobby shown in these contemporary photographs), he proposed arbitration treaties. Negotiations began soon with Britain and France.

of dime novels about an infectiously happy little girl named Pollyanna. But Carnegie's peace rhetoric did not appear for the first time in the deed. Boiler-plate language for him, it showed up in countless speeches, pamphlets, and letters over many years. It reflected his nirvana. His pragmatic agenda was closer at hand.

For most of the trustees who had been part of the arbitration movement, Carnegie's deed, and especially his oral remarks, presumably suggested something still more specific. Carnegie's overwhelming emphasis that day on Taft and arbitration could be seen simply as a reaffirmation of the internationalist frame of mind associated with arbitration for many, many years. Idealistic, yes. Visionary, yes. But grounded in the practical experience that these men shared. Carnegie's emphasis

was for them no surprise, for his own association with the arbitration movement was common knowledge. They could identify readily with Carnegie's arbitration preoccupations. The campaign for arbitration had gone through many cycles; it would go through many more. If the arbitration idea could now be fortified by a new and influential organization, so much the better.

For the trustees in Carnegie's inner circle—and their views naturally were the most crucial—the picture was more complicated. Before them now were important choices to make about their new organization. Their longer-term agendas were not the same as Carnegie's short-term aims on the arbitration front. Nor, however, were these agendas incompatible.

In the short term, as these core trustees probably saw it, the new endowment might well support yet another national push for improving arbitration. Taft had merely made a speech the past March. That speech had to be turned into a policy, that policy turned into a treaty or treaties, those treaty instruments turned into documents that would pass muster in the Senate. How soon and under what precise circumstances these things might happen, none of the trustees could guess. In principle, this board of trustees was proarbitration. So was Carnegie's private agenda.

Meanwhile, in the longer term, these trustees could foresee putting in place, with Carnegie's approval, a much broader scheme of things. Carnegie was willing, even eager, to heed the judgments of his key trustees who advised him that it was important to lay the groundwork for scholarly studies of the economic causes of war, for codification of international law, or for promotion of international dia-

January 24, 1911

Root moves quickly to organize the new institution. A draft legal charter is sent to the founder. Carnegie writes: "I think the proposed charter perfect."

logue. And because he was willing to do this, he approved at the outset the decision to organize the Endowment's work into three operating divisions—dealing with international law, international education, and economics and history—which remained the framework for Endowment programs until after World War II.

This fusion of short- and long-term agendas, at the moment of the Endowment's creation, was plausible and palatable to all concerned. Neither Carnegie nor his trustees could possibly have known that the fusion would be subjected to so much stress so soon, under such unpromising circumstances, or under pressures so volatile and so national in scope.

Carnegie did meet with Taft and Knox at the White House on December 15. Two days later, Taft advanced his arbitration policy a significant step forward—one that Carnegie had hoped for. From the podium at the first annual conference of the American Society for the Judicial Settlement of International Disputes, Taft made an offer: "We must have some method of settling issues between nations, and if we do not have arbitration, we shall have war .... If now we can negotiate and put through a positive agreement with some great nation to abide the adjudication of an international arbitral court in every is-

sue which cannot be settled by negotiation, no matter what it involves, whether honor, territory, or money, we shall have made a long step forward."

At Taft's table that Saturday evening at the New Willard Hotel in Washington sat the French ambassador, Jules Jusserand. As Taft sat down after his speech, Jusserand, according to Taft's biographer, "plucked at the presidential sleeve" and said, "We will make such a treaty with you, if you will make it with us." Taft answered, "I'm your man."

As always, a letter from Carnegie was soon on the president's desk. "Harty congratulations upon your recent speech," he wrote on the twentieth. And as always, there was some advice. This time it was the best he gave Taft during this period, although the president failed to heed it. "Now is the time especially for Sec'y Knox to prepare the ground. I believe if he were to sound the Committee of Foreign Relations in the Senate how your specifics struck them he would be gladly surprised." Soon afterwards, the president instructed Knox to negotiate arbitration treaties "broader in their terms than any ... heretofore ratified, and broader than any that now exist between nations." Britain and France were to be the first candidates.

Six trustees met informally with Carnegie at his home just before the end of the year, and one of them, New York lawyer John L. Cadwalader, was asked by Root to draft the new organization's charter for federal incorporation. Cadwalader had drafted incorporation documents for other major Carnegie institutions. By mid-January Root had appointed a small committee on organization, which included Butler, Choate, and Montague. The committee met promptly to consider Cadwalader's proposed charter. Throughout these discussions, Root was concerned about not giving Congress reason to challenge the incorporation legislation, which Root hoped could be passed in the near future. He wanted a charter neither too specific, lest it arouse opposition from particular interests, nor too general, lest it suggest that the benefaction was so flexible that trustees could do whatever they wanted once incorporated and beyond

A new cop on the beat

Carnegie felt strongly that his new organization should be headquartered in Washington, "under the eye of Root and Scott and at the Ear of Congress."

reach of a Congress suspicious of trusts and big money. The latter concern was heightened by Carnegie's fanciful suggestion that the trustees could decide what evil should be eliminated after war had been abolished; that language, Cadwalader thought, was probably illegal unless qualified.

With Carnegie's participation, Root drafted a general nine-point statement of Carnegie Endowment objectives. The word "arbitration" did not appear in it, and no other potentially controversial subjects were mentioned. On paper, at least, the fusion of agendas seemed a success.

Root's managerial and personal skills were important in the inner circle from the beginning. Root's first disenchanted trustee was Foster, who took Carnegie's arbitration emphasis at face value, and believed that his own long experience with the subject was a special asset to the new organization. Upset over not being named

to the committee on organization, he wrote directly to Carnegie: "It is unnecessary for me to call the attention of one so well informed as you to the fact that I was an active participant in the calling and deliberations of the Arbitration Conference of 1896, the first and most important movement in recent years in the arbitration propaganda, when not a single member of the Committee on Organization took any part in it. I also think my later interest in the cause will not suffer by comparison with theirs." Foster offered his resignation from the board.

Not easily ruffled, Carnegie did the obvious thing. He sent Root to the rescue. About Foster, Carnegie wrote to Scott: "Regret sensitive in mature age, very— and Mr. Foster has been Secretary of State. Pacificator Root should try his delicate hand here." A short time later Scott wrote back, saying he had discussed the Foster matter with Root and that "there is no doubt that he will justify his character of

pacificator and the dispute will not need to be submitted to arbitration." Foster stayed on the board.

Root also sensed at this early date Butler's own independent cast of mind and his wish to preserve his autonomy. Having proposed the previous year that he himself would establish a Washington operation, Butler now argued—presumably because he knew that Root and Scott would be the Washington anchors for the organization, with Carnegie's blessing— that Washington not be regarded as the "principal office" of the Endowment. He said he "feared that the usefulness of the Endowment might be impaired by being permanently located in Washington, because foreigners might consider it as connected in some way or measure with the Government."

Butler, in the months ahead, was to show little reticence about acting on behalf of the White House, but he continued to resist the Washington identification of

In 1911, the Endowment's trustees made their headquarters at 2 Jackson Place in a commodious corner townhouse across from the White House and adjacent to Lafayette Park. This photograph shows the building in 1905, partially hidden by bleachers erected for Roosevelt's inaugural parade.

Carnegie ushers in the new year.

the organization. He wrote Scott that spring from his New York base, "I am more convinced than ever that the Endowment will never amount to much if it is located at Washington." Butler's preference was never shared by Carnegie. "I don't think New York is the proper Hed Quarters," he wrote in 1913 to a fellow New Yorker. "Washington under the eye of Root and Scott and at the Ear of Congress."

February 16, 1911

An acquaintance writes Carnegie: "I have just come from the White House where I had a very interesting talk with the President upon the subject of international peace and your splendid endowment .... I suggested in line with your conversation yesterday that he should now take the initiative in securing from Great Britain a treaty .... I am able to assure you that the president is in accord with your views."

Out of public view, British and American representatives were engaged in preliminary discussions in February. Carnegie wanted faster progress. His impatience showed during exchanges with Scott that month. Carnegie asked how the private talks were going. Scott wrote that the British ambassador had told him that his government was genuinely intent on negotiating a treaty, and he cautioned Carnegie that the information was confidential. Carnegie shot back a handwritten note: "You tell me papers news about treaty, I knew what you tell me long ago." Scott could only reply lamely, "I can give you no information concerning the progress of the arbitration treaty which you do not possess because I have no definite information."

March 17, 1911

Carnegie tells Taft: "The only rock ahed that I see is the opening that Grey's speech give to our opponents here, if we hav any such. I cannot but feel that the sooner a few words from you are given out the better."

British Foreign Secretary Sir Edward Grey had just given Taft's treaty policy a powerful endorsement in the House of Commons. Grey recalled the president's

As treaty negotiations progressed in the spring of 1911, London's Punch magazine portrayed Taft and Foreign Secretary Grey burying the hatchet. Before long, this treaty would greatly preoccupy...

Carnegie, the angel of peace...

arbitration speeches the previous March and December, calling them "bold and courageous." Grey said that Taft "has sketched out a step in advance in arbitration more momentous than anything that any practical statesman in his position has ventured to say before—pregnant with consequences and very far-reaching."

Too far-reaching for the taste of antitreaty forces in the United States, for Grey had implied that an Anglo-American arbitration treaty might well become the basis for a mutual defense pact between the two countries. Carnegie was alert to the danger. When the *New York Daily Tribune,* in a generally proarbitration editorial two days after Grey's speech, observed that public hostility would be intense in America to any alliance, he sent a letter to the editor, telling readers that the Taft policy would produce an arbitration treaty and nothing more. Carnegie sent the published *Tribune* letter to Taft on the seventeenth, with a comment that "the sooner we can nip that thorn the better." In Car-

negie's mind the campaign for the treaty was the president's and his together. "We" and "us" became his standard pronouns.

Taft told Carnegie that there was "no danger of our having an offensive or a defensive alliance." And he reassured Carnegie that "you can count on my going ahead to bring about what we desire. Knox, however, is not here; and I need his suggestive mind to formulate the important words of the treaty." Carnegie waited all of twenty-four hours before writing to Knox, telling him about the "suggestive mind" compliment, and chiding, "Don't be too greatly exalted." Then he diagnosed the situation for the secretary: "I cannot but feel that if the treaty were presented when the Senate meets it would carry all before it, party lines being erased. Notice the British position ... leaders of both parties extolling the idea. This is sublime and we ought to reach this attitude here." Carnegie informed Knox that he had written Democratic party governors "a personal note asking whether they would cooperate with us in elevating the Treaty above partisanship." Next came the typical appeal to history and ego. "Jay's treaty will keep his name in history, but it's a trifle compared to your treaty. . . . What I fear is that if we don't strike while the iron is hot we may fail. We shall de-

serve to do so, but that only aggravates the offense. . . . There is a tide in the affairs of men, etc. Yours has come—now or never."

A few days later, the United Press interviewed Carnegie and reported that "he is in almost daily communication" with Taft. But on the following day Carnegie went too far. After informing Taft that "I was pleased to hear from Senator Root here the other day that he believed the Senate would rise above party and the treaty would not be considered from a party point of view . . . and we know the Senator usually knows what he is talking about," Carnegie started behaving like a secretary of state. He pointed to known concerns that an unconditional arbitration treaty might impinge on purely national matters in countries bound by the treaty, and drafted a model treaty article that he said would satisfactorily take care of that prob-

Taft, the angel of arbitration . . .

and Roosevelt, the angel of nationalism.

Peacemakers Carnegie, Taft, and John Bull are interrupted by German militarism on parade.

lem. An irritated Taft told Knox to rein in Carnegie. Carnegie had already sent off a second model treaty article to Taft. This one was intended to make sure that the president did not renege on his promise to negotiate a treaty that would include matters of national honor. Carnegie pressed Taft—"remember the world will expect to find in the treaty you propose a repetition of the words you used" in the arbitration speeches of 1910.

The secretary sent Carnegie a stern communication sounding almost like an official diplomatic reprimand. "The Government of the United States feels," he cautioned, "as it has reason to believe the British Government does also, that any premature or exaggerated public discussion of this question might perhaps have the effect of disturbing the deliberate study which the two Governments would naturally be compelled to give so important and so difficult a question . . . a question which, I may add, has not yet passed incipient pourparlers between the two Governments."

· Knox's missive chastened Carnegie, at least for the time being. "You know," he reminded Knox, "I am the last man in the world to do anything calculated to impede the great work on which you are engaged, for it is the cause beyond all others I have most at heart and would sacrifice most to advance. I confess," Carnegie admitted revealingly, "I thought it was like most extremely great things, quite easy, the right key to open the door having been found and exhibited by the President, a real open sesame; but after seeing you I may realize that much has yet to be done. So be it! I can be patient."

Carnegie's trustees were now getting organized, meeting in March for the first time as a full board. A charter and bylaws had to be adopted; an executive committee chosen; organizational plans developed for the three divisions; money transferred from Carnegie; and a small operating budget allocated to the new executive committee for interim expenditures.

Requests for money flooded in to the new institution—including one that Scott told his colleagues on the board he placed in his "crank" category. Some fellow, it seems, had written in offering to sell the new peace endowment a million-dollar patent for "a very destructive explosive which he wished us to adopt, which would make war so terrible that nobody would think of resorting to it."

April 6, 1911

Butler learns that the treaty negotiators are close to a successful conclusion. He writes Taft: "I want, within the next thirty days, to put the whole force of the American Branch of the Association for International Conciliation behind a movement to influence members of the Senate . . . ."

Butler sent the president a copy, for approval, of a letter that would go out over Butler's own signature to 30,000 American members of the association. It is not clear whether Butler, who wrote this letter on

"Pax Germanica; or, the Teuton Dovecote." The German eagle says to the "arbitration bird" bearing British and American flags, "No foreign doves required; we hatch our own, thank you." By the end of the spring, Germany had officially refused to negotiate an arbitration treaty.

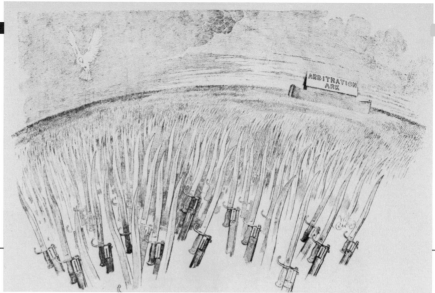

"Back to the Ark. No Refuge for the Dove in All the European Sea."

his Columbia University stationery, discussed this initiative with either Carnegie or other members of the Endowment's board. Butler may have hoped, as did many supporters of the treaty, that quick action on the treaties in the Senate could be secured that spring. In that case, the Endowment would not yet have been well enough organized to get involved. Or he may have known how problematic the specific treaties then being drafted were likely to be for others on the Endowment board—a fact soon to be evident beyond all doubt. Either way, it made no difference. Taft, referring to Butler's ambitious characterization of the terms of the treaty, wrote back the next day: "I doubt the wisdom of your sending out the letter you propose. Just at present I am willing to lie a little low and not make any noise until we have a treaty drafted and presented to the senate."

May 18, 1911

John Morley learns from his friend that the treaty is drafted. Carnegie's telegram reads: "Shake friend Morley, Shake. I am the happiest mortal alive. Couldn't call snakes snake this morning if naming created things."

"Consumate Statesmanship," Carnegie beamed in a note the next day to Taft. Knowing that a treaty would be forthcoming with France as well as Great Britain, Carnegie was particularly pleased, for he calculated that a treaty with Great Britain alone would leave the president most vulnerable to Irish-American opposition. Now, he told the president, "the door wide open for other powers—this silences the few blatant Irish irreconcilables, and paves the way in the Senate. Failure impossible. Favored of the Gods, well, you deserve it. Go up head and stay there six years more."

Two days later came the beginning of the end of the Roosevelt-Taft relationship. It was also the beginning of the end of Andrew Carnegie's personal agenda for the new peace endowment he had created five months earlier.

Roosevelt, on May 20, broke his long public silence about Taft's programs. He opened a frontal attack on what he believed was the most wrong headed and dangerous component of Taft's foreign policy, the arbitration treaties. Even before seeing their text, he wrote a critique in *The Outlook.* This was his first volley in a succession of articles, public and private letters, and speeches that altogether would amount to a slashing personal crusade against the treaties.

The article made clear that Roosevelt was fundamentally opposed to the concept of unconditional treaties. Worse, he believed that the example of such a treaty with England might set a dangerous precedent for American dealings with other nations. Indeed, the snowball effect that proponents of arbitration —including Taft, who evisaged a treaty network embracing eventually Germany, Japan, the Netherlands, Norway, Russia, and Sweden—hoped for from a treaty with England was precisely what Roosevelt wanted to stop.

As he explained to Lodge in a letter written soon after the *Outlook* article: "Of course as regards England ... there is not

August 3, 1911. Britain, France, and the United States sign arbitration treaties. Carnegie cables Taft, "You have reacht the summit of human glory countless ages are to honor and bless your name."

any question that we could not arbitrate .... But with either Germany or Japan it is perfectly conceivable that questions might arise which [we] could not submit to arbitration. If either of them asked us to arbitrate the question of fortifying the Isthmus; or asked us to arbitrate the Monroe Doctrine, or the fortification or retention of Hawaii; or Germany's right to purchase the Danish islands in the West Indies; or Japan's right to insist upon unlimited Japanese immigration—why! we would not and could not arbitrate."

Even though Roosevelt's unmistakably clear letter to Carnegie about arbitration during the kaiser episode had been sent only a year earlier, both Carnegie and Taft believed at first that Roosevelt's challenge was less serious than it really was. Taft wrote to Carnegie: "I am sorry that Theodore thought it necessary to come out in advance of a definite knowledge of what we are trying to do, but I venture to think that what he says is so much aside from the real point that both he and the public will see it, and that it will not interfere with a consummation of what you and I both desire." To Carnegie, Roosevelt wrote in May: "You know that one reason why I hesitated long before writing that

article was just because I hated to do anything that might seem distasteful to you"—a piece of polite sham that must have brought a smile to Carnegie's face— "I finally came to the conclusion that it would be weakness on my part not to write it ... If it had not been for the very unfortunate statement that we would arbitrate questions of honor, I do not think any trouble would have come about the treaty at all."

August 3, 1911

Treaties are signed with Britain and France. The Los Angeles Times *says that no presidential action since the Emancipation Proclamation has been so praiseworthy. The* New York Times *calls the treaties "perhaps the crowning achievement of President Taft's administration." The* New York American *believes, "It will always be remembered of this day—when it has drifted far into the past and become a red-lettered anniversary for universal celebration—that America was the master-spirit that led the way into the new era of peace."*

Historians of the Roosevelt and Taft eras generally agree that the treaties, as one puts it, were "probably the most popular act of the administration in its four years

... and if one can believe the press, an overwhelming majority of all sections of the nation and political faiths was exuberantly commendatory." They also generally agree that the administration's management of the treaties during the negotiating stage and during the ratification debate was a political disaster. The treaties, moreover, were a legal muddle that delighted their opponents and frustrated their defenders.

Compared to ratification debates during the late 1890s and the early 1900s, the forces arrayed on each side in 1911 were unprecedented in their zeal, and the issue engaged the nation more fully than ever before. Roosevelt played the spoiler role, and he played it to the hilt. During the summer of 1911 he and Taft had broken off all personal communication. Roosevelt's decision to challenge Taft for the Republican presidential nomination did not come until early 1912, but the pressures on him to do so mounted steadily during the second half of 1911 and peaked at the end of the year. During these months, he regained the political self-confidence that he had lost at the time of the Republican debacle in the off-year elections of 1910. He now set about to destroy the arbitration treaties and any prospect that they would become the law of the land.

"The Rocky Road to Peace." The cart carrying the arbitration treaties is stuck on the rocks of opposition. Taft and Knox strain to advance the treaties against the resistance of the Senate horse and Foreign Relations Committee Chairman Lodge.

On few other issues during this period of his public life did Roosevelt exert himself so forcefully. As his campaign intensified, so did the superheated, mercilessly aggressive rhetoric that was his hallmark. The "tomfool" treaties were "an act of maudlin folly," and "amiable sentimentality." Roosevelt heaped scorn on the "mollycoddles" who recoiled from defending the national interest with force, and he railed, as he had so frequently in his presidential years, at those naive enough to believe that an "unrighteous peace" was to be preferred to a righteous war. America should not promise to arbitrate when the promise would be false. "In other words," he wrote, "Uncle Sam does not intend to wrong anyone, but neither does he intend to bind himself, if his pocket is picked, his house burglarized, or his face slapped, to 'arbitrate' with the wrongdoer...." To ratify the treaties without amendment "would put the American people in an attitude of peculiarly contemptible hypocrisy.... just as revolting in a nation as in a man."

The treaties represented for Roosevelt a spineless foreign policy. For the hero of San Juan Hill, Taft merely added insult to heresy when he defended the treaties by insisting that if they had been in force earlier the Spanish-American War need not have been fought. A few years later Roosevelt confided to his son Kermit that Taft was "a flabby fool in domestic matters," but an "even flabbier and more incompetent fool in foreign affairs."

Roosevelt's high-decibel attack, however, was not the only novelty in this arbitration debate. More than in any of the earlier senatorial encounters with the issue, the political atmosphere was heavy with raw partisan politics. Before the publication and signature of the treaties, Root's and Carnegie's view that the treaties might well be given bipartisan consideration was fairly widely shared. Even Lodge believed then that his Senate Foreign Relations Committee and the chamber as a whole would have no choice but to endorse the treaties in the end. Evidence was then ample that the treaties would evoke favorable popular sentiment, and although Taft and Knox calculated that lying low was their best strategy, various national advocacy groups organized, demonstrated, rallied, and wrote in support of the treaties as spring turned to summer.

But domestic political considerations were soon to outweigh this early support. Emboldened by Roosevelt's challenge to the treaties, progressive Republicans saw a perfect opportunity to embarrass the Republican Old Guard and Taft. Democrats, aware that Taft had come to see the treaties as a boost to his own sagging political fortunes, and having the 1912 presidential election on their minds, saw an equally perfect opportunity to embarrass the Republicans and capitalize on their crippling divisions.

Senatorial prerogatives—always important in earlier arbitration debates— were now defended more stubbornly, having been treated roughly during the Roosevelt presidency. What most outraged the Senate, though, was the administration's posture of apparent indifference to Senatorial concerns. Consultation had been minimal, even nonexistent at certain critical points. In part this was a calculated risk. Taft and Knox, apparently anticipating resistance from the Senate, did not want to encourage senatorial intervention during the negotiation of the treaties. The administration was heartened by the initial public affirmation of the treaty policy, believing that it would strengthen administration bargaining power with the Senate. In part, however, the absence of consultation stemmed simply from Knox's lack of deftness with the Senate. Furthermore, he sometimes spoke at variance with the president concerning the treaties. He was less convinced an internationalist

With the treaties in jeopardy, Taft takes his case to the people.

than Taft, and probably less committed to the treaties.

August 15, 1911

Henry Cabot Lodge, as chairman, presents the report of the Senate Foreign Relations Committee: "The Committee ... has reported to the Senate, with certain amendments, two treaties ..."

The labyrinthian treaty debate turned on two questions. Should the United States be willing to enter into an unconditional arbitration treaty? And should the United States be obligated to abide by the decision of a joint high commission, formed of nationals from the conflicting countries, empowered to determine whether a particular matter was properly to be regarded as subject to arbitration? On both counts the Senate's majority report answered in the negative. It excluded various categories of disputes from the treaty, and deleted the proposal for a commission, charging that it would strip the Senate of its constitutional authority.

Roosevelt regarded the high commission as the "fatally objectionable feature" of the treaties. For any president to allow a commission to decide whether a matter was properly subject to arbitration, he ar-

gued, "would be proof positive that he was not fit to hold the exalted position to which he had been elected." Roosevelt's barbed conclusion: "A President unfit to make such a decision himself, and willing to have somebody else make it for him, would also be unfit to perform any of the really important duties of the Presidency."

The national controversy that soon swirled around the treaties had few boundaries. The constitutional, legal, and political elements of the debate were all joined; domestic politics and foreign relations intermingled; the symbol and the substance of the treaties merged. And Taft upped the ante as the tide began to turn against him. In a twenty-four-state speaking tour, he stumped for his treaties, much as Woodrow Wilson would do for his League of Nations after World War I.

Taft rebutted the critics on details and conducted what amounted to a running debate with Roosevelt about the philosophy of arbitration and what it meant for the United States. To Roosevelt's charge that the treaties were hypocritical because no nation would submit its important interests to arbitration, Taft answered that avoidance of war required nothing less. Hypocrisy was not the issue; whether arbitration is desirable only for minor problems was not the issue. The issue, Taft

argued, was whether the United States must always get its own way when it comes into conflict with other nations over important interests.

The president elaborated on this theme in one of his early public appeals—delivered the same day the Senate's report on the treaty was released—at a well-known religious camp meeting attended by 12,000 people in Ocean Grove, New Jersey. "We cannot make omelets without breaking eggs," Taft said, "we cannot submit international questions to arbitration without the prospect of losing, and if arbitration is to ... cover the ground that shall really promote the cause of peace and prevent war, it must cover questions of the utmost interest to both countries. ... If the subject of arbitration is merely for discussion in peace societies ... and if the result is not to mean real victory for one party, and real defeat for the other, certainly the time of diplomatic officers ... ought not to be wasted on it. I am very serious in my advocacy of arbitration as a means of settling international disputes, and I believe that you are. I am willing to abide an adverse decision ... for my own country, even though it may impose a serious loss upon her. ... If we are going into the arbitration game, if I may call it such, we must play it through to the end, and

53

we must take our hard knocks with equanimity, as we expect others to take theirs, with the hope and knowledge that the disadvantages that may accrue to each party can never equal the horrible losses, the cruelty and the wickedness of war."

For Roosevelt, arbitration was a potential menace to righteousness; for Taft, it was an affirmation of it. "I believe in arbitration," he declared at Ocean Grove, "to the point that I am willing to arbitrate anything in which I believe I have a good case, and, if I don't believe I have a good case, I wish to give it up in advance of arbitration."

Publicly, Taft took an uncompromising line on the essentials of the treaties, believing that anything less would encourage more obstructionism from the Senate. Predictably, his opponents reacted in kind. Roosevelt had taken the same position regarding his arbitration treaties in 1905, when he had refused to accept Senate amendments. Taft, ironically now doing exactly as Roosevelt had done, reacted to his former mentor's behavior with a mixture of bitterness and sorrow. "It is hard, very hard," this embattled and decent president once remarked to an aide, "to see a devoted friendship going to pieces like a rope of sand."

October 26, 1911

For the first time since signature of the treaties, the Endowment's executive committee meets. Carnegie is present in the morning. The session resumes in the evening, with Carnegie absent. Afterwards, Scott drafts the following passage for the official minutes, but later deletes it: "After careful consideration of the opinion advanced at the morning session and of the attitude of Mr. Carnegie . . . the committee agreed that the work of propaganda begun at the instance of Mr. Carnegie should cease."

Andrew Carnegie abandoned his private agenda for his peace endowment at the end of October, almost exactly a year after he had begun discussions with President Taft. Verbatim transcripts of the executive committee discussion on the twenty-sixth are, unfortunately, not available, but what happened can be credibly reconstructed.

A minority report of the Senate Foreign Relations Committee also had been released in August; Root was the principal author. The report neither endorsed nor criticized the views of Lodge and the majority. In it, Root proposed his own amendment to the treaties, which would limit the presumptive scope of the com-

mitment to arbitrate. This left Root in a generally more pro-treaty posture than the majority, but left him on record, as well, against the unmodified treaty that the president had asked for. For Root, the constellation of personalities involved in the treaty ratification battle was awkward, to say the least, with his valued friends Taft, Roosevelt, and Lodge at the forefront. Worse yet, the Endowment of which he was president had been founded by a man whose views on arbitration in general and the treaties in particular were so well known that Root could not comfortably distance himself from them. With the treaties in the public domain, the question of the Endowment's attitude toward the ratification battle could not be ignored.

Sometime in late September or early October, Butler began preparing for the upcoming meeting of the executive committee. In a draft report to the board on behalf of the division of which he was then acting director, he wrote: "It is the opinion of the acting director . . . that all proper means should be taken by the Division to secure the ratification of these treaties. No effort should be spared to persuade two-thirds of the Senate that the interpretation put upon the treaties by the minority of the Committee on Foreign Relations is correct, and to bring to the sup-

port of that view the public opinion of the country. It may not be amiss to say that Mr. Carnegie himself holds this view very strongly and has urged it with the utmost emphasis upon the acting director."

"There is this technical embarrassment," Butler continued, "in the way of immediate action. Such a campaign as is projected must be organized without a day's delay, and it will be expensive." Butler went on to explain that the small start-up budget that had been authorized by the executive committee the past March was exhausted, but that "Mr. Carnegie ... has authorized the acting director to say to the executive committee that he would advance whatever sums may be thought to be necessary to meet the cost of this campaign, with the understanding that the sums so advanced shall be repaid from the accrued income of the Endowment at the first opportunity." Butler indicated that after consulting with Root, he had "taken steps to set the necessary machinery in motion in the hope of assisting to bring about the prompt ratification of the treaties in December." Finally, Butler drew up a resolution by which the executive committee would authorize him "to arrange for an active campaign," spending an amount "not to exceed $75,000 without further authority from the Trustees."

For these participants in the 1911 Mohonk conference, the arbitration treaties were the prime topic of discussion. Only days before, Roosevelt had opened a public campaign against the arbitration treaties. One of the featured speakers at the conference was John Foster, who reacted strongly to the news of Roosevelt's attack.

"I had concluded the preparation of my address at this point," he told the Mohonk audience, "when the fulmination of Theodore Roosevelt against the proposed treaty appeared in the public press. While I regret its appearance as tending to embarrass the action of the Senate, I recall the fact that no man in public life to-day has shown such an erratic and inconsistent course in relation to the subject of international arbitration. His early public career was marked by a strong hostility to arbitration in general. ...

But when he assumed the responsibility of the presidency, it was he who sent the first case to the Hague court of arbitration, and invited the nations in hostile array against Venezuela to resort to the same court. ...

In 1904 he sent a number of arbitration treaties to the Senate and yet, because that body saw fit to insist upon the exercise of its constitutional duty, he denounced this action as "a sham" and a subterfuge, and in a petulant manner refused to put the treaties into force. But four years later, following the advice of Secretary Root, he sent the same treaties with the Senate's amendment to that body, and upon its approval put them into operation.

Notwithstanding his early declaration in opposition to arbitration in general, he has done more than any other living man to advance this cause and has earned the Nobel peace prize. Judging the future by the past, in the course of time, after he has played to his heart's content with his favorite terms, "hypocrisy," "cowardice," "bad faith," etc., we may expect this erratic but patriotic citizen to fall in line with the onward march towards international peace, and give his support to the great measure which most ennobles the administration of his successor."

In 1911, Taft and Roosevelt drifted toward their final confrontation. The following year, Roosevelt would challenge Taft for the presidency that he had handed to him in 1908.

Roosevelt launched an unrestrained campaign against Taft's arbitration policy in 1911. In this cartoon, "The Spear that Knows No Brother," Roosevelt's "anti-arbitration" javelin finds its mark. Its victim sits in the White House, writing an arbitration treaty.

Roosevelt and Taft stood together at the White House as symbols of Republican unity and continuity in 1909.

None of these passages was ever published as part of Butler's final report in the Endowment's official records. There remains in the Endowment's archives a piece of paper on which is written the resolution that was in fact adopted on the evening of October 26 and that in effect took the Endowment out of the ratification picture. The handwriting is Root's.

With the course of the ratification campaign getting as rocky as it had been in the autumn of 1911, Root judged that Endowment activism on behalf of the treaties, even in the version supported by his own minority report as Butler had suggested, would expose the Endowment and its founder to severe attack. In late 1911, Admiral Mahan, like Roosevelt an outspoken opponent of the treaties, complained loudly about what he called the subsidized agitation in favor of the treaties. The complaint came as the debate was heating up and the Senate was displaying more than its usual animus toward public pressures of this kind. Root must have felt then as he did two years later, when, discussing another matter, he said: "The thing which has made me feel very certain about the importance of keeping out of political matters is that what we do carries a certain prejudice; this is the Carnegie Endowment; Mr. Carnegie is still living, and ac-

tive and prominent. The people of the country are exceedingly sensitive as to the employment of the money of rich men toward influencing public opinion. I think that is the great trouble."

Arguments along these lines would have had strong resonance among the members of the executive committee in October 1911, with a bill of incorporation still pending, with the organization just getting off the ground, and with its founder strongly identified with the most divisive foreign-policy issue of the day. Genuine as these apprehensions might have been, however, more than this was at issue for Root. The arbitration treaties were simply not acceptable to him. He thought the administration's handling of them a disgrace. Indeed, it seems that he was privately more sympathetic to the majority views than he let on publicly. Lodge told Roosevelt, in fact, that Root had helped him write the majority report. Roosevelt believed that Root was more

disposed to seek a compromise position because of his ties to Taft and Carnegie and his wish not to seem as if opposition to the treaties reflected in any way his own pride of authorship in the existing 1908 network of arbitration agreements. Roosevelt, at one point, confided to Lodge, "I saw Root the other day, and he frankly admitted that he was quite as much against the treaty in its proposed form as you were, and was merely trying to break the fall for its backers."

There was something else about the treaty debate that would matter to key members of the Endowment board and to Carnegie himself. The controversy had become a struggle between the president and the Senate. These Endowment trustees all carried a strong respect for the constitutionally based foreign-relations powers of the Senate. For Carnegie, the Senate was a model deliberative institution, its arbitration views notwithstanding. For even the board's strongest proarbitra-

56

But by the 1912 Republican national convention, Roosevelt, brick in hand, was waiting to ambush his former protégé and friend.

Roosevelt, an "irresistible force," meets Taft, an "immovable object."

tionists, the paramount objective was to avoid Endowment entanglement in a challenge to the Senate's constitutional powers.

Foster, for example, who could not attend the October 26 meeting, wrote Root the day before, "I am not informed of the scope of the campaign" being contemplated by the Endowment but "I hope its exponents will not allow it to become an aggressive campaign against the Senate .... that body is made by the Constitution a part of the treatymaking power not only to give its consent to treaties but also to advise in their negotiations. I am informed ... that no member of the Committee on Foreign Relations ever saw a line of the arbitration treaties and no member was consulted by the President or secretary of state before they were sent in. It is almost inconceivable that such a blunder could have been committed. There is nothing left for the Friends of Peace but to advocate their ratification, but we should not oppose reasonable amendments."

According to an internal Endowment history written many decades later, Carnegie had promised Taft early in 1911 that "he would be willing, if necessary, to promote an educational campaign in favor of the ratification of the treaties through the peace organizations with which he was associated." Taft's personal secretary reportedly was then designated one of the president's intermediaries with Carnegie and Butler. Also in the Endowment's archives is an unsigned memorandum, dated October 17, bearing a notation in Butler's handwriting indicating that Taft was the author. It reads: "I am in favor of the treaties as they are, and I hope Dr. Butler and Mr. Carnegie will not fail to press them. ... what I am hopeful of is that the Senate will conclude to compromise on Root's method of ratification, and then if I make that concession, in order to save the Senate's face, it will be a concession which ... will be a sufficient compromise to enable us to let the Senate committee down easily."

Attending the October 26 meeting's morning session were Butler, Montague, Root, Scott, Tower, and Henry S. Pritchett, a long-time intimate of Carnegie's. Most of this group would have agreed with, or deferred to, Root's views on the treaties and on the prudent Endowment posture toward the treaty controversy. The official record of the meeting reveals only that "a thorough discussion of the form and effect of the treaties and the objections which have been raised to them" was held, and that while Carnegie was still present the committee decided to postpone action until the evening session. At the later session, Choate—then vice president of the Endowment but not a member of the executive committee—was also present. The meeting lasted until nearly one o'clock the next morning; the final item on the agenda was Butler's report.

In advance of the meeting, but sometime after Butler had written his draft report, Root and Butler worked out an understanding concerning the Endowment's relationship to the treaty ratification debate. Root's views prevailed, though Butler did not come away empty-handed. On October 10, Butler had set up, outside of the formal structure of the Endowment, a national citizens committee to work on behalf of the treaties. Root consented to the arrangement. The chairman of the group was Choate, presumably Root's assurance that the committee was in good hands. Butler's draft report, which had contained no mention of such a committee, apparently had reached Root sometime before October 10. That was when Butler and Root agreed to a scaled-down program, which included the citizens committee.

At the end of the evening session the executive committee informally gave Butler a go-ahead to continue the organization and work of the citizens committee, whose mandate Butler now described modestly. The committee, he wrote in his amended draft report, would "give moral support to those who are leading the movement for the ratification of the treaties." No resolution of the executive committee was ever passed establishing the committee retroactively or endorsing its work—or even mentioning it by name. Nor did the executive committee specifically identify the Endowment with other

In October 1911, Root persuaded Carnegie that his bargain with Taft could endanger the future of the new peace organization if the Endowment entered the fierce controversy over the treaties.

elements of the modest program that, with Root's knowledge, Butler had been sustaining not only through the citizens committee but through other organiza-

tions with which Carnegie had been associated.

The formal action by the committee, based on Root's handwritten resolution, authorized that Carnegie be reimbursed for sums already expended, but not to exceed $50,000, which was $25,000 less than Butler had asked for in his draft report. The authorization carried the proviso that "no part of such sums are to be used in any controversy regarding the particular form of any arbitration treaty."

That financial ceiling was really tantamount to a cease-and-desist order, as the original but rather infelicitously phrased language of Scott's draft minutes indicated. Butler explained why in a letter written the next day to a colleague involved in running the citizens committee. Before October 26, Butler had already expended or obligated $45,000—all of which he properly assumed would be reimbursed by Carnegie to the Endowment. Now, he wrote, "there remains only a leeway of some $5,000. You will therefore be kind enough strictly to limit the expenditures to the sum appropriated. Parts of the work that have been planned will have to be entirely abandoned; other parts will have to be modified; and the whole movement will have to stop when the $50,000 is expended."

Unforeseen Emergencies

7/1 P73 — *Mr. Carnegie for sums advanced by him for advocating Arbitration Treaties* ... forward 50000

This entry from the Endowment's 1911 ledger records the effect of a key trustee resolution, drafted by Root, that capped funding of protreaty activities. The undoing of Carnegie's political bargain was now official.

Butler also explained in this letter what the official minutes did not reveal. The executive committee had spent "much time" on the matter and Carnegie had "expressed himself very strongly against any activity which could be interpreted as taking the part of the President in any controversy with the Senate over the form of the treaties." The trustees generally felt, Butler reported, that the national controversy over the treaties—Taft's national speaking tour was then a fresh memory—"should not have been permitted to arise at all," and need not have but for "the lack of tact" on the part of the president and Knox. The executive committee's feeling, Butler added, was that the cause of peace and arbitration would be "injured, and not promoted, if a controversy between the President and the Senate is either invited or precipitated."

Root was undoubtedly the key to the outcome of the October 26 meeting. He had persuaded Carnegie that his fledgling Endowment would be damaged if it were caught in the crossfire between Taft and the Senate. He had convinced him that the Endowment's profile in the whole affair should be much lower than Carnegie—and apparently Butler—had originally wanted.

Other members of the board of trustees who were not present on October 26 would have agreed with Root's advice and would have commended their founder's judgment in accepting it. Over the course of the next few years there were occasions for these trustees to comment retrospectively on the Endowment's relationship to the Taft treaties, which for the most part consisted of the efforts of the national citizens committee. They eventually regretted even those circumscribed efforts as an inappropriate intrusion of the organization into political and constitutional controversy. And Root, even though he would later thrust the Endowment into public controversy on other issues, admitted that the association of Carnegie's name with the protreaty voices in 1911 had contributed to continuing congressional opposition to passage of the Endowment's bill of incorporation. (The board eventually gave up the idea of a federal charter, and the Endowment was incorporated in New York State at the end of the 1920s.)

In contrast with Butler's regret over the October 26 decision was Scott's obvious satisfaction. "I believe the treaties are a step backward," Scott wrote to one opponent of the treaties. He said that he was willing to see them ratified "in some shape for the sake of our good faith, which is seriously questioned abroad, but I would regard it as little less than a calamity to have our Endowment, which should be a conservative body, intervene in a conflict between the President and Senate, or to lend its influence actively to secure the ratification.... You will be glad to know that our Executive Committee shares these views, and that at its meeting on October 26 it limited its activity to securing the negotiation of arbitration treaties, but refused to lend itself to the ratification of the present ones, and directed that anybody in its employ, directly or indirectly receiving money from the Endowment, who advocated the cause of the arbitration treaties, should refrain from any expression of opinion regarding the particular form which they should assume."

The full board met at the beginning of December, but by then the Endowment's involvement in the treaty ratification debate had been brought into conformity with the October decision. Butler noted this in his routine report. And in a passing comment, a coda to the whole affair, he reminded the board that "Mr. Carnegie's ideas were, at one time at least, very much larger than this." Among the trustees there was no further discussion. The matter was closed.

Henry Cabot Lodge. His opposition helped turn the Senate into a graveyard for Taft's arbitration treaties.

THE SENATE ACTS

Carnegie did not relent after October in his personal efforts to secure ratification of the treaties. He urged Taft to compromise and take the best deal he could get. He sent the White House textual revisions to the treaty to take account of Senate concerns. He offered advice on political tactics for securing ratification of the amended treaties. Yet Taft remained firm, writing to Carnegie at the end of the year: "I think it wise for us to go for the full treaties as they are. . . . Don't let us give up in advance!"

By then everything that could have been said about the treaties had been said. No other legislative issue in the Taft administration, one historian has written, "occasioned so much letter writing from so many important people." France wanted its treaty, and told Taft not to compromise. Britain did likewise. By all appearances, the American people wanted the treaties as well. A December 1911 protreaty editorial in a New York liberal weekly struck a note of solemnity and realism about the politics of the moment: "This Christmas season is notable because it finds our own great nation calmly deliberating over the precise form of arbitration treaties which would go far to

produce [peace] in the case of any future controversies with the three most powerful nations of Europe. It is well that we should deliberate. The senate, which is soon to become a more democratic body by the popular election of its members, does well to safeguard its constitutional prerogatives. Admiral Mahan does good service in pointing out that diplomacy, with the force which rests upon national efficiency in the background, rather than war alone is to be regarded as the real alternative to universal arbitration. . . . But international arbitration treaties are not so much an alternative as a very natural expression of these ultimate elements in our destiny. We calmly set up international tribunals, not because we are afraid to fight, but because we are strong enough not to fight. We choose to settle disputes by arbitration rather than by the sword because we prefer the kind of justice which arbitration will give us, whether on specific is-

sues we win our case or lose it. . . . it is inconceivable that the treaties should fail. The plain people of the nation who must fight when there is war, who pay taxes when there are war burdens to be met, who suffer when industry is paralyzed, and who share in the blessings of a stable peace and prosperity, have the paramount stake in the outcome of the pending negotiations" between the president and the Senate. "If it is wise national policy and ultimate national efficiency by which we are to be guided let us favor the treaties."

The defeat of the treaties came in March 1912. "The trail of politics," said the *New York Evening Post,* "is over it all." A solid bloc of Democrats plus some Roosevelt Republicans combined to make their opposition decisive. Lodge skillfully led the opposition, using arguments with a familiar ring. For the United States to accept unconditional arbitration would simply encourage others to manipulate trumped-up claims against American interests, he said. "We are tempting, we are inviting, other nations to raise these perilous and vital questions, which now slumber peacefully in a sleep which should know no waking."

Lodge, as he would do later in his historic confrontation with Wilson over the league, now said that he favored the Taft

SENATE RATIFIES TATTERED PACTS

TREATIES, SHORN, PASS SENATE, 76 TO 3

Clause Invading Senate's Rights Is Eliminated and Other Restrictions Are Added.

ROOSEVELTIAN VOTES DECIDE

treaties in principle, and that he would favor them in practice if modified. He then proceeded to use his commanding position in the Senate to strip them of everything that Taft most wanted—notably, the provision for a joint high commission that had become the main bone of contention in the treaty controversy. Carnegie was not alone in urging the president to accept the treaties reported out of the Senate by a seventy-six to three vote as "the best obtainable for the present," not alone in believing—as he had a decade earlier when the Roosevelt package of treaties was similarly altered—that "substantial victory lies in the treaties as they now stand." But presidents humiliated by the Senate are not inclined to be accommodating. Taft, no exception, would write remorsefully some time later about his treaties: "I put them on the shelf and let the dust accumulate on them in the hope that the Senators might change their minds, or that the people might change the Senate; instead of which they changed me."

One month before the Senate's action, Roosevelt had declared that he would challenge Taft for the presidency. The election of 1912 found leading members of the Endowment's board caught up in the struggle that would divide their loyalties, fracture the political party to which

most of them for so long had maintained their allegiance, and pave the way for Wilson's election to the presidency. There was George Perkins, who financed and managed Roosevelt's Bull Moose challenge to Taft. And Straus, who joined Roosevelt, running for governor on the Progressive ticket in New York State and pulling in more votes there than Roosevelt himself, though not enough to win.

Most of all, there was Root himself, in the most tortured political decision of his life, choosing to abandon Roosevelt—not just to abandon him, but to serve as chairman of the 1912 Republican convention, at which Taft was renominated and Roosevelt's delegates were disallowed. Butler helped to write the parliamentary script behind the scenes, and after Taft's vice presidential running mate died near the end of the campaign Butler was designated his successor.

Roosevelt never forgot it. "Root took part in as downright a bit of theft and swindling," at the convention, "as ever was perpetrated by any Tammany ballot box stuffer, and I shall never forgive the men who were the leaders in that swindling." And, in 1913, the unforgiving expresident wrote an autobiography in which Root's name was never even mentioned.

THE POLITICAL BARGAIN UNDONE

Carnegie's political bargain with Taft identified both men with the high tide of early American internationalism, a tide that carried with it a substantial part of the American public. In its simplicity and optimism, it was an internationalism that resided comfortably in the minds of a generation of men like those who sat in the board room of the Carnegie Endowment. Never again in this century would American internationalism seem so capable of being distilled into simple premises about America and the world. Never again would it lend itself to so confident a reliance on international judicial procedures such as arbitration. Never again would it seem so self-evidently sane to so many people in this country.

"Taft lost his fight," one historian has written, but "the nationalists, while they had won a battle, had not won the war for the public mind. They were, in fact, very much on the defensive. An all-out battle on the field of internationalism had been deferred for the moment. . . . And nationalists of the Rooseveltian variety sensed the mounting threat to their positions, implicit in the formation of a new alignment of public opinion."

Root's Republican political voyage and divided loyalties. On the left, Root in 1904 as chairman of the Republican convention, leads the chorus of delegates in "Four years more of Teddy." On the right, Taft gloats as Root, again chairman of the convention in 1912, drives a steamroller over the Roosevelt delegates. The "Three Musketeers" are no more.

Andrew Carnegie has been reduced to many caricatures, some of them deserved. But the cartoon character was not the man who brought a peace endowment into existence in 1910. This was not "Andrew the Cheerful Giver," blithely throwing money at a cause he was drawn to by whim or sheer moralism. Nor was it "Andrew the Manipulated Millionaire," artfully pressed by his friends and advisers until he could no longer resist saying yes to them. Nor was it "Andrew the Angel of Peace," foolishly trying to buy a commodity that could not be bought at any price.

A layman in foreign affairs, Carnegie naturally did not appreciate the intricacies of law or diplomacy. His certainty that important men could do important things easily once they put their minds to it was as wishful as most "great man" theories of history. His rhetoric and tactics reflected his own personality to a fault. His reading of the politics involved in the arbitration controversy was flawed by his congenital optimism—though even his most sea-soned advisers were often as wrong as he was about how the treaty ratification debate might unfold. He angered more people by his persistence and presumptuousness than he should have— the private communications of the day leave no doubt about that.

Yet the story of the Endowment's creation is Carnegie's own story. He was determined to do what he thought was right and necessary. He was determined to do it in his way and at a moment of his choosing. His decision was a typically personal one, and it revealed much about the broad historical context that shaped the great arbitration controversy seventy-five years ago.

The Taft treaties, according to one analysis of the politics of their demise, "brought into the open some characteristically American attitudes toward international relations before the spirit of the nineteenth century was finally overtaken by the events of the twentieth." The anti-treaty nationalists "recoiled from the whole philosophy of international relations which the treaties symbolized, a philosophy that regarded arbitration as much more than an occasionally useful, semijudicial device. . . . Never had this philosophy been more virulent, to their dismay, than during the administration of the

Peace President, as its adherents were pleased to call Taft."

"There were misconceptions on both sides," this same analysis concluded, "neither of which had a monopoly of realism or idealism." This was "because both sides were dealing with a collection of unverifiable ideas at a time when a century of free security and a period of unparalleled peace had given free rein to slipshod thinking about war." The proarbitrationists, in all of their variety, reflected in their tone "the stable, peaceful, but fast disappearing world of the nineteenth century." Roosevelt and Mahan, for their part, "harbored a dangerously mystical conception of war, making it hard to resist the conclusion that they found the idea of preparing for war—and possibly war itself—exhilarating. As exponents of power they were impelled by national egotism rather than by realistic calculations of national security, and they believed that the exertion of power could be controlled, that wars could still be fought for a definite purpose within well-defined limits." There were "few signs in 1911 of poise, of mature national adjustment in Ameri-

At this point the presence of Mr. Carnegie was announced and he was invited to be present at the meeting. It was suggested that it would be a proper time to consider what action the Endowment should take with respect to the pending general treaties of arbitration between the United States and Great Britain and France. After a thorough discussion of the form and effect of the treaties and the objections which have been raised to them, the committee decided to postpone its action until the question came up on the report of the Acting Director of the Division of Intercourse and Education. At the conclusion of the discussion Mr. Carnegie excused himself for the remainder of the meeting.

can attitudes toward foreign policy, plenty of dissension, of gullibility, and of impulsiveness."

Had Carnegie not reached his decision for his own reasons, to pursue his own private agenda, the Endowment may well have never been established at all. Had he not allowed his own agenda to be fused with the longer-term agendas that Root and Butler had assembled, the organization would have lacked the moorings necessary for its work in subsequent decades.

That Carnegie aligned himself as he did in the debate on arbitration should be a surprise to no one familiar with the man and his life. That he wanted to place his peace endowment in the forefront of what he saw as a historic movement toward universal peace should be no surprise either. Least surprising of all was that he

wanted to avoid prejudicing the future of his new institution. Carnegie said once that he did not want to fit the definition of a philanthropist as a man with a great deal of money but very little sense. He agreed to keep the Endowment out of the fierce controversy over ratification when Root told him that it must be done. For this Andrew Carnegie, the decision first to enter the treaty debate, and then to pull back from it, reflected the good sense that he sought to attach forever to his reputation.

In 1935, on the occasion of Carnegie's centenary and the Endowment's twenty-fifth anniversary, Nicholas Murray Butler ranked Root as one of the three men who meant most to Carnegie. In Root, Butler said, "Mr. Carnegie found a calm, cool, detached, sympathetic adviser, a man who shared his enthusiasms but was always

quick to show him their practical limitations and how those enthusiasms could best be harnessed to some organized form or capacity for expression."

Intended as a general characterization of Root's relationship with Carnegie, these words explain, as accurately as any single sentence can, why Carnegie was willing to set aside his private agenda for the Endowment in 1911 and to let his pragmatic instincts override his reformist aspirations. He did so because he trusted Root, and in the remaining eight years of his life he never showed signs of regret for having done so.

Epilogue

ELIHU ROOT remained Carnegie's key adviser on philanthropic matters. He received the Nobel Peace Prize in 1912, continued as president of the Endowment board until 1925, and took special interest in the organization's monumental, 152-volume study of the economic and social history of World War I. Root was told by Mrs. Carnegie late in his life that he had understood her husband "better than anyone else." In 1935, he took part, at age 90, in the commemoration of the Endowment's twenty-fifth anniversary, reminiscing about the days when Carnegie, Butler, and he had collaborated to bring the Endowment into being. Root died in 1937.

NICHOLAS MURRAY BUTLER succeeded Root as president of the Endowment board. He was in charge of the New York office, presided over the Endowment's extensive international research and education programs during the 1920s and 1930s, and received the Nobel Peace Prize in 1931. Butler summered annually in Europe, using as a base the Endowment's imposing Paris headquarters. He became the personification of the Endowment until his retirement from the presidency in 1945, the same year that he stepped down after forty-four years as president of Columbia University. He died at the age of 85 in 1947, the last survivor of Carnegie's original board of trustees.

JAMES BROWN SCOTT remained secretary of the Endowment board and the organization's chief executive officer for three decades after its formation. From Washington, he also headed the Endowment's Division of International Law, bringing it worldwide recognition for promoting study, research and publication in the field. Scott played a leading part in the founding of the Hague Academy of International Law. He retired from the Endowment in 1940 and died in 1943 at age 77.

ANDREW CARNEGIE continued to participate occasionally in board meetings in the years immediately following his establishment of the Endowment. The outbreak of war in 1914 left him profoundly dispirited. "All my air-castles," he said, "have fallen about me like a house of cards." In failing health during the war years, Carnegie lived long enough to welcome the armistice in 1918; he died the next year at age 83. Through his will, he attempted to remedy what he regarded as America's niggardly pensions for its former leaders and their families. He bequeathed an annuity for the widow of Theodore Roosevelt, who had died in the opening days of 1919. Also a prime beneficiary in Carnegie's will was ... William Howard Taft.

Acknowledgments

Two Jackson Place remained the Endowment headquarters throughout the stewardship of Root, Butler, and Scott. It was sold to the U.S. government after World War II, and designated a National Historic Landmark in 1974 because of its association with Andrew Carnegie and the Endowment.

Our excursion into the mind of Andrew Carnegie began at the obvious place— his private papers. His letters and jottings revealed much about his motives in establishing a new peace endowment, and the papers of the other dramatis personae in the story provided additional context and color.

Anne Gibbs mastered these primary sources. Her archival research not only turned up the first important clues about why Carnegie did what he did in 1910, but also became the foundation for our understanding of exactly how he implemented his plan. Her substantive and editorial judgments throughout the project were always well aimed. And her selection of graphic materials enriches nearly every page of this publication.

Amanda Cadle made certain that draft after draft of the manuscript was produced on schedule, overcoming severe deadline pressures, sometimes indecipherable copy, and a word-processing system that seemed occasionally to possess an uncooperative mind of its own.

Others helped with production at critical junctures, notably, Sara Goodgame, Catherine Jay, and Renée Key. Peter Lavoy provided an assist with the preparation of notes. David Weiner initially tracked down important sources for graphic materials in Washington and New York. Leslie Weinfield patiently proofread the manuscript several times. Copy editor Joan Berne met her usual professional standards despite having to contend with Carnegie's quirky spelling and punctuation.

As always, Jane Lowenthal and her staff at the Endowment's remarkably responsive library were indispensable; indeed, Jenny Grimsley, Patricia Sheehan-Burns, and Monica Yin probably learned more about Carnegie sources than they ever wanted to know. The staff at the Rare Book and Manuscript Library of Columbia University gave an extra measure of help during our effort to extract what we needed from the Endowment's archives on deposit there.

For overall guidance, special thanks go to Tom Hughes, whose keen and informed interest in the origins of the organization he heads sparked this project in the first place. His commentary on successive drafts sharpened the history and enlivened the prose. Sanford Ungar's practiced instincts as an editor challenged us to keep the story simple, the writing clear, and the personalities vivid. His advice and judicious prodding have produced welcome improvements at every stage.

L.L.F.

Notes

page

3 *"Private.* I have . . ." Carnegie to Morley, 4 November 1910, Andrew Carnegie Papers, Library of Congress (hereafter ACLC).

3 "I do not see . . . tainted thereby." Burton J. Hendrick, *The Life of Andrew Carnegie* (Garden City, N.Y.: Doubleday, Doran & Co., 1932), 2:337.

3 Carnegie asked them both . . . Carnegie to Knox, 29 November 1910, ACLC.

4 Carnegie also wanted . . . Carnegie to Taft, 8 November 1910, ACLC.

4 "The trouble with old Carnegie . . ." *Taft and Roosevelt: The Intimate Letters of Archie Butt, Military Aide* (Garden City, N.Y.: Doubleday, Doran & Co., 1930), 2:557.

5 "Constitution of Carnegia . . ." Maxwell H. Bloomfield, *Alarms and Diversions: The American Mind through American Magazines, 1900-1914* (The Hague: Mouton & Co., 1967), 52-53.

6 John D. Rockefeller's favored . . . "like to know?" Edward Chase Kirkland, *Dream and Thought in the Business Community, 1860-1900* (Ithaca, N.Y.: Cornell University Press, 1956), 2-3.

6 "really a tremendous personality . . ." *Autobiography of Andrew Carnegie* (Boston and New York: Houghton Mifflin Co., 1920), 340n.

6 "in his ambition . . ." Mark Sullivan, *The War Begins, 1909-1925,* vol. 4 of *Our Times: The United States, 1900-1925* (New York: Charles Scribner's Sons, 1932), 140.

7 "The more I see . . . his reputation." Meeting of the Board of Trustees, 14 December 1910, verbatim transcript, 10-11, Carnegie Endowment Archives at Columbia University (hereafter CECU).

7 "I would walk . . ." Sullivan, *Our Times,* 4:498.

7 Roosevelt regarded Root . . . Roosevelt to Carnegie, 18 February 1910, in Hendrick, *Life of Andrew Carnegie,* 2:327.

7 "a great man . . ." *Autobiography of Andrew Carnegie,* 275.

7 "looks like a piece . . . discussion." *Letters of Archie Butt,* 1:151 and 2:693.

8 "The personality and character . . ." Richard W. Leopold, *Elihu Root and the Conservative Tradition* (Boston: Little, Brown and Co., 1954), 173-174.

8 "Incapable of panic . . ." William H. Harbaugh, *The Life and Times of Theodore Roosevelt,* rev. ed. (New York: Oxford University Press, 1981), 125-126.

8 Root one-liners taken from Jessup, *Elihu Root,* I:363, 254, 453, 191; Root to Butler, 8 March, 1909, Butler Papers, Columbia University.

9 "In virtue of my interest . . . wise and feasible." Carnegie to Trustees, 14 November 1910, ACLC.

9 "On the one side . . ." Henry Steele Commager, *The American Mind* (New Haven: Yale University Press, 1950), 41.

9 "The United States . . . is seated . . ." Ernest R. May, *Imperial Democracy* (New York: Harper & Row, 1961), 242.

12 "Being a lawyer . . ." William Allen White, *Masks in a Pageant* (Westport, Conn.: Greenwood Press, 1971), 330.

12 "I have noticed exceptions . . . attractive the audience." William Howard Taft, speech before the American Peace and Arbitration League, New York City, 22 March 1910, William H. Taft Papers, Library of Congress (hereafter WHTLC).

13 "the great jewel . . ." *Letters of Archie Butt,* 2:635.

14 "No words from any Ruler . . ." Carnegie to Taft, 26 March, 1910, ACLC.

14 "the solution came unexpectedly . . ." *Century Magazine,* June 1910.

15 "taught the world Arbitration." George A. Finch, "History of the Carnegie Endowment for International Peace, 1910-1946" (Carnegie Endowment, Washington, D.C., Mimeographed, n.d.) 4.

15 "England and [the] United States . . ." David Patterson, *Toward a Warless World: The Travail of the American Peace Movement, 1887-1914* (Bloomington: Indiana University Press, 1976), 18.

15 *"Race,"* Carnegie wrote . . . Andrew Carnegie, *The Gospel of Wealth and Other Timely Essays,* ed. Edward C. Kirkland (Cambridge, Mass.: Belknap Press of Harvard University Press, 1962), xiv.

15 "perhaps best expressed . . ." Patterson, *Toward a Warless World,* 19.

15 "I think the twentieth century . . ." Howard K. Beale, *Theodore Roosevelt and the Rise of America to World Power* (Baltimore, Md.: Johns Hopkins University Press, 1956), 81.

15 "the Anglo-Saxon race . . ." C. Roland Marchand, *The American Peace Movement and Social Reform, 1898-1918* (Princeton, N.J.: Princeton University Press, 1972), 33.

15 "God has not been preparing . . ." Richard Hofstadter, *Social Darwinism in American Thought,* rev. ed. (Boston: Beacon Press, 1955), 180.

16 "metaphysician of the homemade intellectual," ibid., 32.

16 "Here," he proclaimed, "are my . . ." Hendrick, *Life of Andrew Carnegie,* 1:240.

16 "not an accident . . ." Hofstadter, *Social Darwinism,* 40.

17 "the whole world owes . . ." Elihu Root, *Addresses on International Subjects,* ed. Robert Bacon and James Brown Scott (Cambridge: Harvard University Press, 1916), 39.

17 "I believe in arbitration . . ." Marchand, *American Peace Movement,* 35.

18 "practically sovereign," Samuel Eliot Morrison, Henry Steele Commager, and William F. Leuchtenburg, *The Growth of the American Republic* (New York: Oxford University Press, 1980), 2:241-242.

19 "war with the United States . . ." May, *Imperial Democracy,* 48.

19 "the sudden appearance of Germany . . ." *The Education of Henry Adams: An Autobiography* (Boston: Houghton Mifflin Co., Sentry Edition 3, 1961), 362-363.

19 "like competitive examinations . . ." May, *Imperial Democracy,* 52.

20 "one of the greatest events . . ." Patterson, *Toward A Warless World,* 39.

20 "arbitration had been in the air . . ." John Dos Passos, *Mr. Wilson's War* (Garden City, N.Y.: Doubleday & Co., 1962), 13.

21 "Remember the *Alabama* . . ." Patterson, *Toward a Warless World,* 20.

22 "As to arbitration . . ." *Autobiography of Andrew Dickson White* (New York: The Century Co., 1905), 2:259.

22 "It should teach us . . . battleships." Beale, *Theodore Roosevelt,* 91. See also p. 41.

23 "Important though it is . . ." ibid., 337.

23 "Such is the opinion . . ." Joseph Frazier Wall, *Andrew Carnegie* (New York: Oxford University Press, 1970), 922.

24 "fear quite as much . . ." Beale, *Theodore Roosevelt,* 349.

24 "Personally I think that . . ." ibid.

24 "it does not represent . . . practicable." ibid., 349-350.

24 "dominated solely by . . ." ibid., 340.

24 "intense interest . . ." *Arguments and Addresses of Joseph Hodges Choate,* ed. Frederick C. Hicks (St. Paul, Minn.: West Publishing Co., 1926), 640.

25 "In a good cause . . ." Philip C. Jessup, *Elihu Root* (New York: Dodd, Mead & Co., 1938), 2:82.

25 "the arbitration business . . ." Warren F. Kuehl, *Seeking World Order: The United States and International Organization to 1920* (Nashville, Tenn.: Vanderbilt University Press, 1969), 113.

25 "secured the attention . . ." H. C. Phillips, *A Decade's Review of the Lake Mohonk Conference on International Arbitration, 1895-1905* (Mohonk Lake, N.Y., 1904), n.p.

26 "War does not often settle . . ." Charles William Eliot, "International Arbitration," in *American Contributions to Civilization and Other Essays and Addresses* (New York: The Century Co., 1898), 381.

27 "Dear Sir and Friend . . ." *Autobiography of Andrew Carnegie,* 295.

27 "Didn't you feel . . . it's his money." Wall, *Andrew Carnegie,* 865.

27 "Carnegie was tired . . . under." ibid., 881.

28 Mr. Dooley excerpts taken from Gail Kennedy, ed., *Democracy and the Gospel of Wealth* (Boston: D.C. Heath, 1949), 114; Beale, *Theodore Roosevelt,* 351; Elmer Ellis, *Mr. Dooley's America: A Life of Finley Peter Dunne* (Archon Books, 1969), 246.

29 "If we could only . . ." David S. Patterson, "Andrew Carnegie's Quest for World Peace," *Proceedings of the American Philosophical Society* 114 (20 October 1970): 376.

29 Another suggestion . . . "my funds." Ginn to Carnegie, 19 January 1907, ACLC.

30 "Where did this damn . . ." Nicholas Murray Butler, *Across the Busy Years: Recollections and Reflections* (New York: Charles Scribner's Sons, 1939), 1:316.

31 "By persistent public demonstrations . . ." Charles Herbert Levermore, *Samuel Train Dutton: A Biography* (New York: Macmillan Co., 1922), 93-94.

32 "I infer that . . ." Butler to Carnegie, 8 January 1909, ACLC.

32 "It is a matter that . . ." Carnegie to Butler, 11 January 1909, ACLC.

32 "If any peace or arbitration . . ." Carnegie to Benjamin Trueblood, 5 February 1908, ACLC.

32 "I think on the whole . . . anyone else." Holt to Butler, 14 January 1909, ACLC.

32 "with a view to . . ." Butler to Carnegie, 6 April 1909, ACLC.

32 The proposed institute . . . pursuit of justice. "Proposed Plan for the Establishment of a Carnegie International Institute," enclosed with Butler to Carnegie, 6 April 1909, ACLC.

33 "You are the most important . . ." Butler to Root, 27 January 1910, Nicholas Murray Butler Papers, Columbia University.

34 "Do you know . . ." Hendrick, *Life of Andrew Carnegie,* 2:303-304.

34 "a little Hague Conference of his own." ibid., 325.

34 "There is really your Big Game," ibid., 326.

35 "The fact is . . ." ibid., 321-322.

35 "Ah, I see! . . . abreast." ibid., 314.

36 "Neither Root, Butler . . ." ibid., 326.

36 "With *your* policy . . ." ibid., 327.

36 "My past words . . ." ibid., 327-328.

36 "The crux of . . ." ibid., 328-329.

37 "I shall use both . . ." ibid., 330.

37 "I think that friend Root . . ." Carnegie to Roosevelt, 18 April 1910, ACLC.

37 "through some inadvertence . . ." *The Letters of Theodore Roosevelt,* ed. Elting E. Morrison (Cambridge: Harvard University Press, 1954), 7:377.

37 "If, as I suppose . . ." Hendrick, *Life of Andrew Carnegie, 2:331.

37 "I would establish . . ." Butler to Carnegie, 8 April 1910, ACLC.

38 "simple, economical, and would . . ." Butler to Carnegie, 8 April 1910, ACLC.

38 "the usual dissentions . . . go on conquering." Carnegie to Roosevelt, 18 April 1910, ACLC.

39 "the exact form . . ." Frederick Lynch, *Personal Recollections of Andrew Carnegie* (New York: Fleming H. Revell Co., n.d.), 155.

39 "That will give . . ." Taft to Carnegie, 28 October 1910, WHTLC.

39 "Teddy, come home . . ." Sullivan, *Our Times,* 4:441.

39 "The difference between . . ." Jessup, *Elihu Root,* 2:164.

40 "I do not see . . ." Roosevelt to Root, 21 October 1910, Elihu Root Papers, Library of Congress.

40 "I believ that the shortest . . ." Carnegie, draft Deed of Trust, 3 November 1910, ACLC.

40 "all of them are . . . you return." Carnegie to Taft, 8 November 1910, ACLC.

40 "Personally, I should like . . . a treaty." Carnegie to Knox, 11 November 1910, ACLC.

40 "Have decided upon . . . easy to arrange." Carnegie to Roosevelt, 16 November 1910, ACLC.

41 "No part of this fund . . . given." Carnegie, draft of Deed of Trust, 3 November 1910, ACLC.

41 "It seems so clear . . ." Carnegie, draft Deed of Trust, 5 November 1910, ACLC.

41 "even Senator Root . . ." Carnegie to Scott, 22 November 1910, ACLC.

41 Carnegie's board of trustees . . . Knox to Carnegie, 28 November 1910, ACLC.

41 "It is splendid . . . I sent" Carnegie to Knox, 29 November 1910, ACLC.

41 "changed my views . . ." Carnegie to Knox, 30 November 1910, ACLC.

42 "I . . . have read . . ." Taft to Carnegie, 11 December 1910, ACLC.

42 "After talking with Mr. Root . . ." Knox to Carnegie, 4 December 1910, ACLC.

42 "The President . . ." Root to Carnegie, 7 December 1910, ACLC.

42 "the action of the trustees . . ." ibid.

42 "You will note . . . Ruler to declare." Carnegie to Taft, 10 December 1910, WHTLC.

43 ". . . I know beyond all question . . . knows it all." "Mr. Carnegie's Address to the Trustees," *Year Book of the Carnegie Endowment for International Peace, 1911* (Washington, D.C.: C.E.I.P., 1912), 5-6.

43 The members of the Endowment's original board of trustees not mentioned prominently in the text are:
Robert S. Brookings: merchant and philanthropist
Thomas Burke: chief justice of the Territory of Washington
Cleveland Dodge: merchant and banker
Arthur William Foster: railroad president and banker
Austen G. Fox: lawyer
Robert A. Franks: financial associate of Carnegie's

William M. Howard: Democratic congressman from Georgia
Samuel Mather: mining company president
George W. Perkins: partner, J.P. Morgan Co.
Henry S. Pritchett: president, Massachusetts Institute of Technology
Jacob J. Schmidlapp: banker
James L. Slayden: Democratic Congressman from Texas
Charles L. Taylor: business partner of Carnegie's
John Sharp Williams: Democratic senator from Tennessee
Robert S. Woodward: astronomer and geologist

43 "hasten the abolition . . . banishment," "Mr. Carnegie's Letter to the Trustees (Deed of Trust)," ibid. 1-4.

45 "We must have . . . " *Proceedings of International Conference under the Auspices of American Society for Judicial Settlement of International Disputes, December 15-17, 1910* (Baltimore: The Waverly Press, n.d.), 352-53.

45 "plucked at the . . . I'm your man." Henry F. Pringle, *The Life and Times of William Howard Taft* (1939; Hamden, Conn.: Archon Books, 1964), 2:739.

45 "Harty congratulations . . . gladly surprised." Carnegie to Taft, 20 December 1910, WHTLC.

45 "broader in their terms . . ." George E. Mowry, *The Era of Theodore Roosevelt and the Birth of Modern America, 1900-1912* (New York: Harper & Row, 1958), 278.

45 "I think the proposed . . ." Carnegie's marginal notation on letter from Scott to Carnegie, 24 January 1911, ACLC.

46 "It is unnecessary . . ." Foster to Carnegie, January 1911, ACLC.

46 "Regret sensitive . . ." Carnegie's marginal notation to Scott on letter from Foster to Carnegie, January 1911, ACLC.

46 "there is no doubt . . ." Scott to Carnegie, 31 January 1911, ACLC.

46 "principal office . . . Government . . ." Meeting of the Committee on Organization, 21 January 1911, verbatim transcript, n.p., CECU.

47 "I am more convinced . . ." Butler to Scott, 10 May 1911, CECU.

47 "I don't think New York . . ." Carnegie's marginal notation on letter from R. Johnson to Carnegie, n.d., in files of Carnegie Endowment.

47 "I have just come . . ." William Morrow to Carnegie, 16 February 1911, ACLC.

47 "You tell me papers news . . ." Carnegie to Scott, 10 February 1911, CECU.

47 "I can give you . . ." Scott to Carnegie, 11 February 1911, CECU.

47 "The only rock ahed . . ." Carnegie to Taft, 17 March 1911, WHTLC.

48 "bold and courageous . . . ." Sir Edward Grey, Address before the House of Commons, 13 March 1911, *Parliamentary Debates* (Commons), page 1989.

48 "the sooner we can . . ." Carnegie to Taft, 17 March 1911, WHTLC.

48 "no danger of our . . ." Taft to Carnegie, 17 March 1911, WHTLC.

48 "you can count on . . ." Taft to Carnegie, 20 March 1911, WHTLC.

48 Carnegie waited . . . "now or never." Carnegie to Knox, 21 March 1911, ACLC.

48 "he is in almost daily . . ." United Press interview, 24 March 1911, WHTLC.

48 "I was pleased to hear" . . . rein in Carnegie. Carnegie to Taft, 25 March 1911, with file memo, WHTLC.

49 "remember the world . . ." Carnegie to Taft, 27 March 1911, ACLC.

49 "The Government of the United States . . ." Wall, *Andrew Carnegie,* 983.

49 "You know . . . can be patient." Carnegie to Knox, 28 March 1911, ACLC.

49 "a very destructive explosive . . ." Meeting of Board of Trustees of the Carnegie Endowment, 9 March 1911, verbatim transcript, 55, CECU.

49 "I want, within the next . . ." Butler to Taft, 6 April 1911, Butler Presidential Papers, Columbia University.

50 "I doubt the wisdom . . ." Taft to Butler, 7 April 1911, ibid.

50 "Shake friend Morley . . ." Wall, *Andrew Carnegie,* 984.

50 "Consumate Statesmanship . . . six years more." Carnegie to Taft, 19 May 1911, WHTLC.

50 "Of course as regards England . . ." Harbaugh, *Life and Times of Roosevelt,* 377.

51 "I am sorry that Theodore . . ." Taft to Carnegie, 20 May 1911, WHTLC.

51 "You know that one reason . . ." Wall, *Andrew Carnegie,* 985.

51 The *Los Angeles Times* . . . "Taft's administration." John P. Campbell, "Taft, Roosevelt, and the Arbitration Treaties of 1911," *Journal of American History,* September 1966, 280.

51 "It will always be remembered . . ." "A Crushing Blow to the Black Barbarism of War," *New York American,* 14 August 1911, Philander C. Knox Papers, Library of Congress.

51 "probably the most popular . . ." Mowry, *Era of Roosevelt,* 278.

52 "tomfool . . . wrongdoer . . ." Campbell, "Taft, Roosevelt, and Arbitration," 284-85; Pringle, *Life and Times of Taft,* 2:744; and Theodore Roosevelt, "The Peace of Righteousness," *The Outlook,* 9 September 1911, 70.

52 "would put the American . . ." Pringle, *Life and Times of Taft,* 2:751.

52 "a flabby fool . . ." Campbell, "Taft, Roosevelt, and Arbitration," 279.

53 "The Committee . . ." U.S. Congress, Senate Committee on Foreign Relations, *Report on the General Arbitration Treaties Signed with Great Britain and France,* 62nd Cong., 1st sess., 25 August 1911, 3.

53 "fatally objectionable feature . . . Presidency." Roosevelt, "The Peace of Righteousness," 69.

53 "We cannot make omelets . . . . advance of arbitration." "Taft Intimates Appeal to People," *New York Times,* 16 August 1911, 4.

54 "It is hard . . ." Pringle, *Life and Times of Taft,* 2:753.

54 "After careful consideration . . ." Meeting of the Executive Committee, 26 October 1910, draft, n.p., CECU.

54 "It is the opinion . . . authority from the Trustees." Annual Report of Division of Intercourse and Education for 1911, draft, n.d., CECU.

55 Excerpts from Foster's Mohonk speech taken from Address of Hon. John W. Foster, "Unlimited Arbitration between Great Britain and the United States," in *Report of the Seventeenth Annual Lake Mohonk Conference on International Arbitration, May 24th, 25th, and 26th, 1911* (Lake Mohonk Conference on International Arbitration, 1911), 124.

56 "The thing which . . ." Meeting of the Board of Trustees, 17 April 1914, verbatim transcript, 77-78, CECU.

56 "I saw Root ..." Jessup, *Elihu Root,* 2:273.

57 "I am not informed ..." Foster to Root, 25 October 1911, CECU.

57 According to an internal ... "down easily." Finch, "History of the Carnegie Endowment", 1:79, 81.

57 "a thorough discussion ..." *Minutes of the Meetings of the Board of Trustees and Executive Committee, Carnegie Endowment for International Peace,* 1:115.

58 "give moral support ..." *Year Book of Carnegie Endowment,* 1911, 71.

58 "no part of such ..." *Minutes,* 1:125.

58 "there remains only a leeway ... precipitated." Butler to Loomis, 27 October 1911, CECU.

59 "I believe the treaties ... should assume." Scott to Turner, 6 November 1911, CECU.

59 "Mr. Carnegie's ideas ..." Meeting of the Board of Trustees, 14 December 1911, verbatim transcript, 88, CECU.

60 "I think it wise ..." Taft to Carnegie, 29 December 1911, WHTLC.

60 "occasioned so much ..." Mowry, *Era of Roosevelt,* 279n.

60 "This Christmas season is notable ..." "Social Forces," *The Survey,* (2 December 1911):1268.

60 "The trail of politics ..." *New York Evening Post* in *Current Literature,* April 1912, 375.

60 "We are tempting ..." ibid., 377.

61 "the best obtainable ... now stand." Carnegie to Taft, 2 April 1912, WHTLC.

61 "I put them on the shelf ..." Patterson, *Toward a Warless World,* 180.

61 "Root took part in ..." Harbaugh, *Life and Times of Roosevelt,* 431.

61 "Taft lost his fight ..." Robert Endicott Osgood, *Ideals and Self-Interest in America's Foreign Relations: The Great Transformation of the Twentieth Century* (Chicago: University of Chicago Press, 1953), 97.

62 "brought into the open ..." Campbell, "Taft, Roosevelt, and Arbitration," 279.

62 "recoiled from the whole philosophy ..." ibid., 287-88.

62 "There were misconceptions ... impulsiveness." ibid., 297.

63 "Mr. Carnegie found ..." Nicholas Murray Butler in *Andrew Carnegie Centenary, 1835-1935* (New York: Carnegie Corporation, 1935), 55.

64 Root was told ... Jessup, *Elihu Root,* 2:488.

64 "All my air-castles ..." Hendrick, *Life of Andrew Carnegie,* 2:345.

PHOTO AND GRAPHIC CREDITS

3, *Andrew Carnegie,* courtesy of the Library of Congress; 4, *Taft and Root,* Library of Congress; 4, *Philander Knox,* Library of Congress; 5, *entry from cash journal,* photo by Chad Evans Wyatt; 6, *J.P. Morgan,* courtesy Library of Congress; 6, *Carnegie mansion,* Photo Library Department, Museum of the City of New York; 9, *John Foster,* Library of Congress; 9, *Andrew White,* Culver Pictures; 9, *Oscar Straus,* Library of Congress; 9, *Joseph Choate,* Library of Congress; 9, *Luke Wright,* U.S. Army Center of Military History; 10, *Charles W. Eliot,* Library of Congress; 10, *Albert Smiley,* Mohonk Mountain House; 10, *Andrew J. Montague,* Robert L. Montague; 12, *Taft speaking,* reprinted by permission from The Hearst Corporation. Copyright ©1911 The Hearst Corp. All rights reserved; 13, *Carnegie dictating,* Culver Pictures; 15, *William Tell cartoon,* New York Public Library Picture Collection; 15, *Albert Beveridge,* Library of Congress; 16, *Herbert Spencer,* Culver Pictures; 18, *Grover Cleveland,* Library of Congress; 20, *Olney-Pauncefote Treaty,* photo by Chad Evans Wyatt; 21, *Hague photo,* courtesy Library of Congress; 22, *Alfred Thayer Mahan,* Library of Congress; 23, *Roosevelt as Caesar cartoon,* New York Historical Society, New York City; 24, *Lake Mohonk,* Mohonk Mountain House; 25, *1905 Lake Mohonk Conference,* Mohonk Mountain House; 26, *Mark Twain,* Culver Pictures; 28, *board room, Carnegie Institution,* Carnegie Institution of Washington; 29, *Carnegie Instutution,* Carnegie Institution of Washington; 30, *Nicholas Murray Butler,* Columbia University, photo by Chad Evans Wyatt; 31, *Mr. Carnegie's Room,* courtesy Photo Library Dept., Museum of the City of New York, photo by Richard Averill Smith; 35, *Roosevelt with rhino,* courtesy Culver Pictures; 35, *Kaiser,* Library of Congress; 36, "*Medal to the Only Peaceful Monarch,*" Culver Pictures; 37, *Roosevelt and Kaiser on horses,* Culver Pictures; 43, *Carnegie at desk,* Culver Pictures; 44, *Pennsylvania Ave. scene,* Library of Congress; 44, *Willard Hotel, exterior,* Library of Congress; 45, *Willard Hotel, lobby,* Library of Congress; 49, *Taft as angel,* New York Public Library Picture Collection; 49, *Carnegie, Taft and John Bull at peace table,* reprinted by permission from The Hearst Corporation. Copyright ©1911 The Hearst Corp. All rights reserved; 51, *treaty signing ceremony,* reprinted by permission from the Hearst Corporation. Copyright ©1911 The Hearst Corp. All rights reserved; 53, *Taft speaking from train,* Library of Congress; 54-55, *1911 conferees at Lake Mohonk,* Mohonk Mountain House; 56, *Roosevelt and Taft,* Library of Congress; 58, *Elihu Root,* Library of Congress; 59, *entry from ledger,* photo by Chad Evans Wyatt; 60, *Henry Cabot Lodge,* Culver Pictures; 62, *Root at 1904 Republican convention,* Culver Pictures.

DESIGN: SCHUM & STOBER, GRAPHIC DESIGN, INC.